# Answers TO Science Questions

## FROM THE Stop Faking It! Guy

# Answers to Science Questions

## FROM THE Stop Faking It! Guy

William C. Robertson, PhD
Illustrations by Brian Diskin

National Science Teachers Association

Arlington, Virginia

National Science Teachers Association

Claire Reinburg, Director
Jennifer Horak, Managing Editor
Judy Cusick, Senior Editor
Andrew Cocke, Senior Editor
Wendy Rubin, Associate Editor

SCIENCE AND CHILDREN
Chris Ohana, Editor
Monica Zerry, Managing Editor
Valynda Mayes, Associate Editor

ART AND DESIGN
Will Thomas Jr., Director
Tim French, Senior Graphic Designer, cover and interior design
Brian Diskin, cover art

PRINTING AND PRODUCTION
Catherine Lorrain, Director

NATIONAL SCIENCE TEACHERS ASSOCIATION
Francis Q. Eberle, PhD, Executive Director
David Beacom, Publisher

LIBRARY OF CONGRESS CATALOGING-IN-PUBLICATION DATA
Robertson, William C.
  Answers to science questions from the stop faking it! guy / by William C. Robertson ; illustrations by Brian Diskin.
    p. cm.
  Includes bibliographical references and index.
  ISBN 978-1-935155-24-9
  1. Science- Miscellanea. I. Title.
  Q173.R63 2009
  500--dc22
                              2009025256

eISBN 978-1-936137-99-2

*NSTA is committed to publishing material that promotes the best in inquiry–based science education. However, conditions of actual use may vary, and the safety procedures and practices described in this book are intended to serve only as a guide. Additional precautionary measures may be required. NSTA and the authors do not warrant or represent that the procedures and practices in this book meet any safety code or standard of federal, state, or local regulations. NSTA and the authors disclaim any liability for personal injury or damage to property arising out of or relating to the use of this book, including any of the recommendations, instructions, or materials contained therein.*

*Featuring sciLINKS®—a new way of connecting text and the Internet. Up-to-the minute online content, classroom ideas, and other materials are just a click away. For more information go to* www.scilinks. org/faq/moreinformation.asp.

# Contents

# Physical Science

# Technology

# Index

# Introduction

What you have in your hands is a collection of columns I wrote for the journal *Science and Children*. Each month the editors and I tried to choose a science question befitting the particular theme of that month's issue. As a result, I cover a wide variety of topics. There is a small amount of overlap with the content of the *Stop Faking It!* books, but not much. That's to be expected, because writing a book is completely different from writing a column.

My task as a book author is to put together a number of concepts in a coherent pattern, with one concept building on the previous concepts. With a column, I take one interesting question and explain the science behind that single question. Of course, the column brings different challenges: As I tackle subjects less familiar to me than others, I often have to do some research prior to writing. I find plenty of discussions of these concepts in books and on the internet, though few of them are any good, and I must wade through the sometimes jargon-laden explanations to get the real story of what's going on. For example, I knew the basics of photosynthesis, but I wanted a complete view of the process from an energy perspective. That wasn't easy when the articles I read contained as many as 10 new vocabulary words per paragraph—words that didn't help with understanding! All of this is to say, I do the heavy lifting to help teachers like you get the information you need in a concise, and readable, format.

Prior to my taking on the column as a regular gig, the Science 101 space was filled by a variety of science types. After my first few columns, though, the editors asked me to continue writing it because we worked well together, and heck, it was fun. Writing this column presents exciting learning opportunities. I thought I knew why a curveball curves, for example, but after doing the research, I discovered that it is more complicated (and interesting) than I originally thought. In another column I was surprised to find out that it is, in fact, possible to turn graphite into diamonds. Superman wasn't so far off after all!

To that end, I thank Chris Ohana, Monica Zerry, and Valynda Mayes for giving me this opportunity, for a great working relationship, and for their insightful comments and suggested changes. They helped me see where my explanations weren't clear, and they stopped me—more than once—from going too far over the top and possibly from offending people, even though what got cut was pretty darned funny, I thought! In other words, they saved me from myself.

In most of these columns, I try to replicate what I do in the *Stop Faking It!* books, which is to explain concepts by having the reader complete simple activities *before* diving into the explanations. That process helps most people improve their understanding, so I recommend you actually do the activities rather than just read through them. Trust me, the effort will pay off in helping you "get it" *and* should give you ideas for use in the classroom.

You get an extra bonus in this collection—a Brian Diskin cartoon for *each* column. I only wish you could see the cartoons he developed that we couldn't use, because they're all funny. You also get stupid puns and lame jokes from me, but that's not new if you're familiar with my other work.

I should say something about the title of this book. On the rare occasions when people recognize me at conferences, I sometimes get the question, "Hey, aren't you the *Stop Faking It!* guy?" It's nice to be known for something, even if people don't remember my name.

Anyway, I hope you enjoy this collection and learn a few things while you're at it. I know I learned a lot in the research and writing of the columns.

—Bill Robertson

# General Science

# Q: What writing represents what scientists actually do?

A: Often the writing that students in elementary school do in connection with science is their final report of a science fair project. They diligently file a report in the form of the *scientific method*—introduction, hypothesis, materials, procedure, results, and conclusion. This form of science writing persists through college courses in science, and it isn't unusual for someone majoring in a science discipline to have lab reports as his or her main writing product in science. Of course, one must do a paper or two based on researching and understanding a particular topic in science, but that's usually the extent of writing that ventures beyond reporting labs.

This situation brings up a couple of questions. The first is whether or not a

Topic: Science Writing
Go to: www.scilinks.org
Code: ASQ001

report based on the scientific method accurately represents what scientists do. The second is what kind of writing scientists engage in that goes beyond the reporting of conclusions. I'll try to address those questions in this column. And no, I won't be providing a list of ideas for science fair projects! I know that's a major concern, but it's a topic for another column. For now, just tell 'em to do a baking soda and vinegar volcano (joking!).

## First Do, Then Write

Does the reporting of science using the scientific method really represent how scientists do science? The short answer is no. Scientists seldom follow the scientific method, even though the reporting of experiments in scientific journals more or less follows that template. The question that follows is, "Okay, smart guy, what procedure *do* scientists follow?" To understand that process, it might help to consider what most kids do when they get a new video game. Do they read the instructions? Nah. They familiarize themselves with the controls and just start playing. They mess around with the game for a while and see what happens. Only then do they go back to the instructions to learn a few things. The instructions make a whole lot more sense once you are somewhat familiar with the game.

Scientists do something similar to what kids do when they first play a video game. Scientists "mess around" a bit with the subject matter. Of course, messing around in science isn't exactly the same as messing around with a video game. Messing around in science means you become familiar with the research already done in your area, and

it means trying out a few experiments (or thoughts, in the case of theoretical science) just to see what happens. You might even try to reproduce what others have done to hone your skills. The main point is, until you become familiar with what you're studying, you can't begin to formulate a hypothesis. Formulating a hypothesis often is a first step in the scientific method, but it is not the first step in doing science.

Just a quick note about how scientists proceed from the point of formulating a hypothesis. A scientist might start with a particular question to investigate and soon realize that the original question was the wrong one or that the original question has led to a more intriguing question. A scientist who is truly interested in his or her field of study soon has more questions than he or she can answer in a lifetime. This is one of the reasons why scientists take on research assistants to help accomplish goals. Plus, graduate assistants are a cheap source of labor!

## "Talking" Results

It would be pretty boring if all of science writing involved nothing more than people publishing the results of their experiments. Thankfully for us, that's not all they do. The "scientific community" wouldn't put up with that, anyway. When you make a claim of an experimental result or alteration of a scientific theory, you can expect that others in your discipline will scrutinize your work, looking for errors in procedure or errors in the logic that led you to your particular conclusions. Most science journals publish not just original research but also responses from other scientists to that research. A back-and-forth conversation regarding relevant issues is not uncommon.

A good example of this was the "discovery" of cold fusion a number of years ago. The original research publication on cold fusion sparked a whole bunch of articles in which scientists mostly refuted the original results. Without this written criticism, we would not now know that cold fusion was an unfulfilled dream.

Some of the more interesting historical science artifacts are letters written back and forth between prominent scientists who disagreed on various theories, from the theories of electricity and magnetism to the theories of quantum mechanics. With increased publication in national journals, the increased ease of mobility of scientists, and the presence of the internet, such personal written correspondence among scientists is not as common as it was 100 years ago, but such correspondence established the need to be able to communicate one's ideas and to be able to criticize others' work in a coherent way.

## Communicating Concepts

One of the most important uses of writing in science is to communicate the concepts of a discipline to both future scientists and laypeople. Textbooks are one obvious means of doing this, but we should also include synopses of major science ideas intended for the general public as well as magazine and newspaper articles that convey general ideas and recent discoveries.

Although some people who might not be active in research specialize in translating scientific concepts for lay-people, practicing scientists also contribute in this area. Stephen Hawking's books provide an insight into how his mind works; James Watson's *The Double Helix* is a great book that not only explains his and Francis Crick's investigations into DNA, but gives a glimpse into the excitement of scientific discovery.

## Science Writing for Students

Okay, so what does any of this suggest with respect to students writing while doing science? One obvious place to introduce science writing is in the presentation of science fair projects. Instead of having classmates ask a few questions of the presenter, have them choose one project and write a formal critique of the procedure, results, and conclusion. Where was the procedure particularly good or particularly flawed? Does the conclusion follow logically from the results? You can use this process to teach students how to be critical while not biting the head off the experimenter!

In the realm of reporting science to the public, you could have students compose a column for the school newspaper or bulletin that briefly explains what your class has been doing in science and what conclusions you've reached. You could circulate this column in your class for review and comment prior to submitting it to the school.

Finally, there's the old standby of having kids do a report on some scientific subject. Although it's perfectly okay to have the students report on the adaptations of the red fox or the rings of Saturn, keep in mind that these kinds of reports are not typical of what practicing scientists do. It might be worthwhile to spice up students' science writing with some of the other alternatives suggested in this column. Now, here's how to create the perfect vinegar and baking soda volcano … ■

## Resource

Watson, J. 2001. *The double helix: A personal account of the structure of DNA.* New York: Touchstone.

# Q: When drawing graphs from collected data, why don't you just "connect the dots"?

Anyone who has asked students (including adult students!) to draw a line (or curve) that represents actual data is familiar with the tendency of students to draw a line that touches every single data point. For example, let's say your class has the exciting task of determining how the length of a frog's hind legs affects how far the frog can jump. Suppose the graphed data look like Figure 1 (p. 8). (Note: I'm making up this data—I have no idea if the data would represent the linear relationship suggested by Figure 1.) Then you ask the students to draw a line that represents the trend evident in the data. More than likely, they'll give you something like Figure 2 (p. 8).

"Yeah, it *could* be human error, **or** ... the test subjects are trying to communicate!"

At this point, try drawing a straight line that shows the general trend of the data but doesn't pass through each data point, as in Figure 3.

Perhaps after a lengthy conversation with the students, you can convince them that the data suggest a *linear* relationship, meaning that as the length of a frog's legs doubles, the distance it can jump doubles; as the length of a frog's legs triples, the distance it can jump triples; and so on. If you then ask the students why—if indeed this is the relationship between leg length and jumping ability—don't all of the data points lie exactly on the line you drew, a common answer will be that it's because of "human error." Although this might be true in some cases, there is an "error" in any measurement due to the limitations of the measuring instruments. When measuring using a ruler marked off in centimeters, for example, you have to estimate to, say, the nearest tenth of a centimeter. To represent this inherent uncertainty in a measurement, scientists add *error bars* to the data points, as indicated in Figure 4. Using error bars on graphs is a good way to help students see that within the inherent uncertainty of the measurements due to the instruments used for measurement, the data points do, in fact, lie along the line that represents the linear relationship.

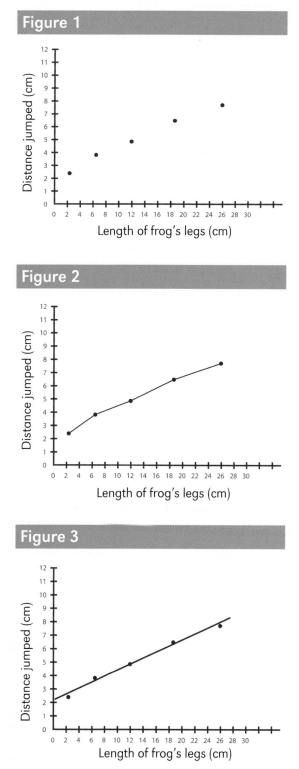

Figure 1

Figure 2

Figure 3

## Figure 4

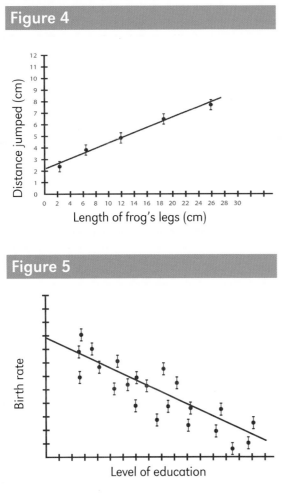

## Figure 5

explain why all the data points do not fall along the line if that line is supposed to represent the relationship between birth rate and education (twice the level of education, half the birth rate; three times the level of education, one third the birth rate, etc.). The answers were varied, as I am sure the answers will be if you ask the same question of your students. The most common answer is, again, "human error," as if the science itself is perfect and the only thing that can keep the graph from being perfect is humans messing it up. Other answers include that some countries don't keep accurate counts of birth rates or don't have any way of keeping track of the amount of education. Such anomalies should already have been taken care of in plotting the data and in determining the error bars. It takes a lot of coaxing for the students to realize that other factors (variables) have an effect on the birth rate in a country. These factors include religion, income level, and the laws of the country. In other words, since there are many things affecting birth rate besides education, it would be silly to expect the collected data in our graph to fall exactly on a straight line even though the data suggest a trend of a straight line. The same is true for our frog example. By considering only the length of a frog's legs, we are ignoring the thickness of the legs, the weight of the frog, the shape of the frog, and any prior jumping training (joke) that might affect how far that frog can jump.

## Uncertainty Doesn't Explain It All

Let's switch gears and look at a graph (made this one up, too) that shows the relationship between the birth rate and the level of education for various countries around the world.

In Figure 5, each data point represents the numbers from a different country. Note that the data suggest a linear relationship, even though it's impossible to draw a line through the data that falls within all of the error bars. I have actually asked students, using a graph similar to this one, to

## It's All About Trends

Whether it's because of uncertainty due to measurement or the lack of consideration of other variables, it is unrealistic to expect collected data to give a graph that describes an exact mathematical relationship—that all the points will fall exactly on a certain line or curve that represents a particular mathematical formula. Rather, what we should look for are general trends in the data. With enough experimental data and repetition, it's possible that these general trends can suggest or confirm exact mathematical relationships. The bottom line, though, is that the trends that lead to more exact relationships are not going to be obvious if all we do is connect the dots on graphs of collected data. You might end up with a drawing that looks vaguely like a bird or a snake, but not something of scientific value. ∎

Topic: Data Collection, Display, and Analysis
Go to: *www.scilinks.org*
Code: ASQ002

# How is reading science books different from reading other kinds of books?

One short answer to this question is that for many people, there *is* no difference. My wife and I make a good case study for different ways of reading books. Being the nerd I am, I try to analyze such everyday things as different reading speeds and look for a reason. First, here's the difference between our reading styles: My wife can read a novel in about half the time it takes me to read the same novel. Within a year's time, she can pick up the same novel and read it a second time. Me, I read novels once and consider reading one a second time a tedious task.

Explaining the difference in our reading speeds is pretty simple. I've spent a good deal of time reading science books. My wife's experience is primarily in

"It's a romance novel. Stop analyzing it."

Topic: Reading and Writing
in Science
Go to: www.scilinks.org
Code: ASQ003

history and political science reading. A good history book tells a story, much like a good novel. In reading those stories, one is able to read through the text relatively quickly and still get the main points. Science reading is a much slower process. You read science texts to understand specific concepts, and usually few of the words on a page are wasted; just about every word can be significant for understanding the concept at hand. Suffice it to say that my wife has a difficult time with science texts, while I'm so slow I never get through history texts.

## The Research Says So

Backing up this view of science reading is a fair amount of psychological research. For example, there are lots of studies that compare experts (those who have studied or even taught a subject for a long period of time) and novices (those new to a subject) in many areas. One of the earliest such studies was done in chess (Chase and Simon 1973). The researchers found that experts organized their knowledge of chess in a fundamentally different way from how novices looked at the game. The experts saw patterns the novices didn't see and organized their knowledge in "chunks"—large collections of chess-piece positions and possible moves arising from those positions. Similar studies in science problem solving reveal that experts have a rich connection of science concepts and a knowledge of the important features of problems, while novices tend to focus on a problem's surface features, which are often unimportant, when considering how to

solve that problem (Chi, Feltovich, and Glaser 1981).

For example, it's common for novices to classify problems as a "spring problem," an "elevator problem," or a "pulley problem." Experts, on the other hand, classify problems according to the major principles—Newton's second law, conservation of energy, conservation of momentum—one uses to solve the problems. So, novices often see details but not the big picture, while experts see the big picture and use the details as necessary.

## Reading Like an Expert

Well, how do you become an expert and see the big picture? You have to understand the important concepts, know all of the subconcepts that are related to the important concepts, and keep everything in the proper hierarchy. Surprise, surprise—this takes time! To develop this richly connected understanding of concepts, you need to read explanations slowly, reflecting on what you have read and how it fits into what you already know. Personally, I can easily spend an hour ruminating over a page or two of reading that covers a particularly difficult science concept. As I ruminate, I ask myself questions, such as "How does this new material fit in with concepts I've already learned?" and "Are there any real-world experiences to which this material applies?" Perhaps the most important question, though, is "Does this make sense to me?"

An example I often use in teacher workshops is the second part of Newton's first law, which states that objects in motion tend to keep moving in a straight line unless acted upon by an external force. I challenge people to provide an everyday example of a thing moving in a straight line without slowing down or stopping. Of course, there *isn't* an everyday example of this, unless you're an astronaut who spends a lot of time in the space shuttle. To understand this part of Newton's first law and have it make sense to you, you have to understand how Galileo (not Newton) came up with this concept. With a couple of other people, I wrote an article on this for *Science and Children*, and I'll refer you to that for an explanation (Robertson, Gallagher, and Miller 2004). But I digress ... back to the main point, which is that if the science you're reading about doesn't make complete sense to you, then you are unlikely to add it to your collection of science concepts that do make sense. You'll either leave the new concepts as unconnected ideas that you are likely to forget, or you'll simply memorize the new concepts and make them last awhile before you then forget them. And again, making sure the concepts make sense takes more time than reading the material as if it were a novel.

## It Takes More Than Reading

Of course, reading alone isn't the best way to learn science (Robertson 2006/2007). You need to connect the reading to real-world experiences. Interposing activities and reading helps people understand concepts better, but only if they go slowly enough in the reading to make the connections between activity and concept.

Adding to the slow reading you have to do with science books is the fact that the pages often contain equations and series of equations. To understand what the author is doing, you have to follow his or her math steps, and that takes time. Some books are really good at helping you follow these equations, and others are really good at letting you figure it out on your own. Ironically, some authors seem to believe that the more difficult the material, the less the need for explanation of the equations. ∎

## References

Chase, W. G., and H. A. Simon. 1973. Perception in chess. *Cognitive Psychology* 4:55–81.

Chi, M. T. H., P. Feltovich, and R. Glaser. 1981. Categorization and representation of physics problems by experts and novices. *Cognitive Science* 5:121–152.

Robertson, B. 2006/2007. Getting past "inquiry versus content." *Educational Leadership* 64 (4): 67–70.

Robertson, W. C., J. Gallagher, and W. Miller. 2004. Newton's first law: Not so simple after all. *Science and Children* 41 (6): 25–29.

# Q: Why do we classify things in science?

Each year, in thousands of classrooms across the country, students classify animals, rocks, and other things as part of their science studies. Each year, thousands of students no doubt ask, "Why in the heck are we doing this?" Classifying things according to their properties and characteristics is a big part of science, but what's the purpose? Why do it in science class, and why do scientists do it as part of their work?

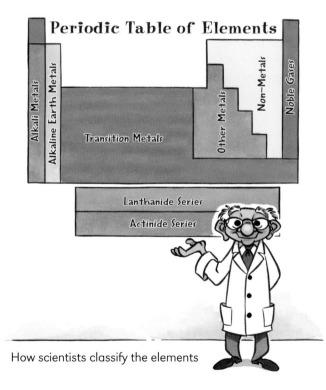

How scientists classify the elements

## Careful Observation

An activity that's been around a long time is to give a group of students a handful of peanuts. Each student chooses a peanut and writes a detailed description of the peanut. The students put the peanuts back in the original pile and then trade descriptions with other students. Then the students match the description they have with one of the peanuts in the pile. This activity helps students learn the skills of observation and communication, skills that are important when doing science. Also, it's just plain fun to do. Unfortunately, though, much of science instruction doesn't get beyond observing, communicating, and classifying. For example, it's common for students in Earth science classes to classify rocks according to their luster, hardness, etc., and then move on to other subjects. A first step in chemistry often is for students to memorize the location of elements on the periodic table. And of course biology students know the pains of memorizing the kingdoms and phyla of lots of different organisms. Do we do these things in the classroom because they're inherently interesting? Unlikely. At any rate, the peanut activity I refer to here has been around awhile, which is why I used it as an example. If you would like to try this activity with students, make sure none of your students are allergic to peanuts.

## Classifying for a Purpose

In her first week of chemistry, my daughter came home and asked me to help her by identifying the line on the periodic table between metals and nonmetals. I asked her what the difference was between metals and nonmetals, and of course she didn't know. We were even, because I didn't know offhand where that line was between metals and nonmetals.

Chemists classified different elements and came up with the beginnings of the periodic table before they had an understanding of the underlying structure of elements. The organization of the periodic table was important, however, as a prelude to this understanding, which we call *atomic theory*. Once you know something about the way in which protons, neutrons, and electrons come together to form atoms, the periodic table has a whole new meaning.

How students classify the elements

I'll discuss what this implies for teaching kids about chemistry in a bit. For now, we can look at other ways that classifying has helped scientists develop a deeper understanding of the world.

When physicists took on the entertaining task of smashing different particles into one another, they found that they produced a whole bucket load of new subatomic particles. What caused the production of these new particles, and how did they fit into our theory of atoms? As a first step toward answering these questions, physicists began classifying the new subatomic particles according to properties they could observe, such as *charge, mass, charm,* and *strangeness.* (Yes, these are actual properties—who says scientists aren't whimsical?) With the classification schemes, they were able to develop a theory of "quarks," and later "strings," which can explain the original classification and give us new insights into the structure of matter.

On to Earth science. As with the previous examples, geologists classify rocks to further their understanding. Knowing what kinds of rocks are found at different locations of the Earth, one can determine the processes that might have formed the rocks and thus piece together a history of the formation of the Earth's features. Engineers also use the classification of rocks and soils to predict the behavior of these rocks and soils when you begin moving them around and using them for various structures.

## In the Classroom

As I said in the beginning, classification for the sake of classification can be fun and useful, but I wouldn't recommend it as a steady diet. It always helps to have a reason for doing the classification. Let's take taxonomy in life sciences as an example. Suppose you have students memorize the kingdoms and phyla of various organisms simply because that's what you do in life science. Suppose also that after this memorization, you move on to studying ecosystems. Does knowing the aforementioned taxonomy help you understand ecosystems? Not much. It would be better to classify organisms as herbivores, carnivores, and omnivores prior to studying ecosystems. That way, construction of food chains as an understanding of the energy flow in ecosystems makes a lot more sense.

In chemistry, should you have students memorize the periodic table, or portions thereof, prior to investigating the structure of atoms? Yes, if your purpose is to help students understand the historical development of chemistry. No, if your purpose is to have students use the periodic table to predict what happens when different elements come together. Once students know how electrons fill energy levels, the periodic table becomes a convenient method for viewing what different atoms look like and knowing what they are likely to do when they encounter other atoms. Why memorize the table before knowing the atomic structure that underlies the overall organization? For that matter, why memorize the table at all?

To close, here are a few simple guidelines for the use of classification in science classrooms. Classification for the purpose of building observation and communication skills is okay, but on a limited basis. Be wary of using classification simply because it's what scientists do. Classification in the classroom should lead toward the understanding of concepts, or at least should be done with an eye toward the ultimate purpose, such as the classification of rocks leading toward an understanding of the formation of geologic features. Finally, even though classification might have historically preceded understanding, as with the periodic table, the historical approach might not be the best way for students to understand important concepts.

And with those recommendations, I'll file this column under "the nature of science." Or should I file it under "interdisciplinary science"? How about according to "date created"? Or maybe according to how close I was to missing the deadline. ∎

**SCILINKS**
THE WORLD'S A CLICK AWAY

Topic: Classification
Go to: www.scilinks.org
Code: ASQ004

# Do balances and scales determine an object's mass or its weight?

A number of years ago, I began to notice in science activities and lesson plans that people referred to the process of "massing" objects instead of "weighing" them. That trend continues today, so maybe we better get it straight. Do you *mass* objects, *weigh* objects, or do something else to them when you're using a balance or a scale? To answer

that, I'm first going to have to explain the difference between mass and weight.

## Mass Versus Weight

The typical elementary-school explanation of the difference between mass and weight goes something like the following: Mass is the amount of matter contained

"Are you sure you're measuring my weight and not my mass?"

in an object. If you travel to the Moon, another planet, or anywhere far away from Earth, your mass doesn't change. Weight is how hard Earth pulls on you. When you travel to the Moon or another planet, the pull of gravity changes, so your weight changes. Personally, I never found this definition of mass and weight to be satisfactory. The explanation is correct, but I don't travel to other planets a whole lot, and neither do students. It turns out there is a much more complete explanation of the difference between mass and weight, but it requires that you understand one of Newton's famous laws of motion.

Newton's second law deals with changes in motion and what causes those changes. We use the term *acceleration* to refer to any change in an object's motion. Whenever an object changes its speed and/or direction, the object has accelerated. Thus, objects speeding up, objects slowing down, and objects moving in a circle (change of direction) are all accelerating. *Forces*—the name we give to pushes, pulls, whacks, nudges, and tweaks—are what cause changes in motion *(accelerations)*. Everyday experience tells us it's more difficult to change the motion of some objects than it is others. A force applied to a large boulder will change the boulder's motion less than the same force will change the motion of a pebble. How difficult it is to change an object's motion is called the object's *inertia*. Inertia is not a force. Inertia is the tendency of an object to remain in its current state of motion. So, forces can cause an object to accelerate, but inertia, not being a force, cannot cause an object to accelerate.

Finally, *mass* is a numerical measure of an

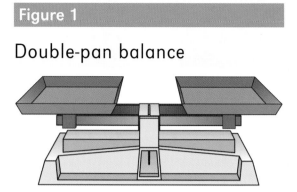

# Figure 1

# Double-pan balance

object's inertia. The more inertia something has, the larger the number assigned to its mass. Thus, mass and inertia are essentially the same thing. The only difference is that mass has a number associated with it. Of course, this formal definition of mass relates well to the definition of mass being a measure of the "amount of stuff" in an object. The more matter in an object, the more difficult it is to change the object's motion, and the greater the mass. The less matter in an object, the less difficult it is to change the object's motion, and the smaller the mass. It's easier to change the motion of a Ping-Pong ball than it is to change the motion of a golf ball. This is reflected by the fact that the Ping-Pong ball has a smaller mass than the golf ball and also has less matter in it than a golf ball.

Newton's second law ties all of this information into one simple equation. If you add together all of the forces acting on an object, taking the direction of the forces into account (this is referred to as the *net force*), that number is equal to the mass of the object multiplied by its acceleration.

(net force acting on an object) = (mass of object) (acceleration of object)
or
$F = ma$

Here's a simple example of Newton's second law in action. Suppose a box with a mass of 10 kilograms is sitting on a frozen pond (we can assume that there are no friction forces on a frozen pond). You exert a force of 20 Newtons (Newtons are the unit of force in the metric system of units) sideways on the box. What is the acceleration of the box? To find out, we just use $F = ma$. The force is 20 Newtons and the mass is 10 kilograms. So,

$$F = ma$$
$$20 \text{ Newtons} = (10 \text{ kg}) \cdot a$$

It's no major math feat to figure out that the acceleration, $a$, is equal to 2 meters per second squared. Okay, the 2 is easy, and you'll just have to take my word for it that meters per second squared are the correct units to use here.

Now, *weight* is *defined* as the force the Earth exerts on an object. *Mass* is *defined* as a measure of an object's inertia. This makes the distinction between mass and weight clear. Weight is a force, and it goes on the left-hand side of $F = ma$. Mass is a measure of inertia, and it's the $m$ that goes on the right-hand side of $F = ma$.

So how can you directly determine the mass of an object? You have to exert a net force on it and measure the resulting acceleration, then use $F = ma$ to determine the mass. For example, suppose you have a rock of unknown mass. You exert a force of 40 Newtons on it, and you measure the resultant acceleration to be 10 meters per second squared (there are many ways to measure acceleration). Then Newton's second law applied to the rock looks like this:

$$F = ma$$
$$40 \text{ Newtons} = m \cdot (10 \text{ m/s}^2)$$

Solving for $m$ gives you a value of 4 kilograms. Exert a force on something, measure its acceleration, and you can solve for its mass.

## Scales and Balances

Scales and balances don't measure accelerations, so clearly they don't measure mass in the way I described above. What do they do? Let's start with an easy one—bathroom scales. You step on the scale, and it tells you your weight. Of course, some scales will tell you your mass in kilograms, so that might be confusing. But it's pretty obvious that the scale is reacting to how hard you are pushing on it. That's a force. To check that the scale is responding to forces rather than mass, have someone push down on the scale while you're standing on it. Most bathroom scales use a spring to measure the force exerted on them. Whatever the mechanism, clearly bathroom scales measure weight, not mass.

Let's move on to a double-pan balance. For those of you with faulty memories, Figure 1 shows a double-pan balance. The way you use this is to put the object to be weighed (or is it massed?) on the left pan, and then add objects of known mass or weight to the right pan until it balances.

Are you comparing the mass of the thing on the left to the mass of the thing on the right, or are you comparing the forces these objects exert on the balance? Again, all you have to do is push down or up on one of the sides to see that you are comparing forces. If you push down on the right pan, does the effect on the scale depend on the mass of your finger or on how hard you push? Yep, it's how hard you push. Thus, a double-pan balance compares the force exerted on the left pan with the force exerted on the right pan. Without meddling fingers involved, the forces exerted by the objects are the weights, not masses, of the objects. So a double-pan balance measures weight.

Finally, let's discuss something a bit trickier—triple-beam balances, shown in Figure 2.

To operate a triple-beam balance, you place the object to be weighed on the pan, and then adjust the *position* of the weights on the right until things balance. By the way, the scales at your local gym or doctor's office operate the same way. You do not add or subtract weight to or from the right side, but rather change the position of the weights. Clearly, then, a triple-beam balance doesn't measure force directly. You adjust a triple-beam balance until the *torque* (defined below) applied by the object on the left balances the torque(s) applied by the weights on the right. The torque exerted on something depends not just on the force applied, but also on the position at which you apply the force. Torques cause objects to change their state of rotational motion, as opposed to forces that cause objects to change their state of linear motion. When the torques on a rotating object (our triple-beam balance) are equal and opposite, the object balances. So, a triple-beam balance directly measures torque, not force or mass.

## How Do We Get Mass?

If we use scales and balances to determine weight or torque, how do we end up with

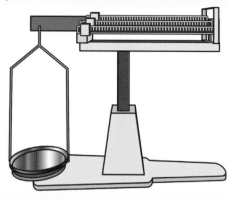

### Figure 2

# Triple-beam balance

readings in units of mass? Well, it turns out that there is a very special relationship between an object's mass and its weight when the object is near the surface of the Earth. To figure out that relationship, consider an object that's falling to the Earth. If we ignore air resistance (physicists make simplifying assumptions all the time), then the only force acting on the object is the pull of gravity. Newton's second law tells us the following about an object being acted on by the force of gravity only:

(net force acting on the object) = (mass of object) (acceleration of object)

Force of gravity = (mass of object) (acceleration of object)

We already know that the force of gravity acting on an object is defined as the object's weight. What you might also know is that all objects near the Earth's surface have the same acceleration when the only force acting is gravity. There's a special symbol for that acceleration, which is *g*. The value of *g* is 9.8 meters per second squared. Using this knowledge, we can now write Newton's second law for our falling object as

(weight of an object) = (object's mass) • $g$

In other words, an object's weight is equal to *mg*. Armed with this relationship, we can measure the weight of an object (using a spring scale or a balance) and then mathematically determine the mass of the object (because we know the value of *g*). Scales and balances are calibrated so the calculation is automatically done and you can read mass directly on the scale or balance, even though the thing being compared or measured is either weight or torque.

So what's the verdict? Do you *weigh* objects or *mass* them? Technically, you *weigh* them because scales and balances measure or compare forces, with triple-beam balances being the exception in that they use torques. If you read the mass of objects directly on the scale or balance, though, you can be forgiven if you claim that you are "massing" the object. Just be aware that the only way to truly "mass" an object is to exert a force on it and measure the resulting acceleration. Also be aware that any comparison between mass and weight involves a conversion, both numerically and conceptually. They are not the same thing.

I'm sure there's a great joke to end with regarding being torqued off, but at the moment it escapes me. In lieu of that, I'll add a note for the purists out there. I have been talking about what is known as *inertial mass*, so named because of its role as a measure of inertia. There is another type of mass, though, known as *gravitational mass*, which is the mass that is responsible for the gravitational force (or curvature of space-time, if you wish!) exerted by all objects that have mass. To put your mind at ease, to date no one has been able to determine a numerical difference between inertial mass and gravitational mass. Don't lose any sleep over it, okay? Doesn't it just torque you off when someone gives you a patronizing comment like that? ■

Topic: Mass/Weight
Go to: *www.scilinks.org*
Code: ASQ005

# How does a scientific theory become a scientific law?

A theory *doesn't* become a law. End of story. Just kidding—it's all about the *how* and *why*, and that hasn't been answered. I'd like to step back a bit and address a common misconception that unfortunately permeates science education. See if this sounds familiar: Scientists begin with a *hypothesis*, which is sort of a guess of what might happen. When the scientists investigate the hypothesis, they follow a line of reasoning and eventually formulate a *theory*. Once a theory has been tested thoroughly and is accepted, it becomes a scientific *law*. Nice progression, and not what happens. To understand how scientists proceed in their investigations, it will help to understand each term individually. What's a *hypothesis*, what's a *theory*,

"Look, kid, *I* don't know why. Ask *him* to explain it!"

and what's a *law*? I'll deal with these in reverse order.

## The Law of Laws

To understand what a law is, you just have to look at various laws in science. Boyle's law states that when the temperature of a gas is constant, the pressure of the gas times the volume of the gas is always a constant, regardless of how the pressure and volume change. The law of conservation of mass in chemistry says that the total mass of the things that react together is equal to the total mass of the things that are produced in the reaction. Newton's second law states that the net external force applied to an object is equal to the mass of the object times the acceleration of the object. These things are called *laws* because every time people have tested them, they hold true.[*]

But let's examine what laws do not tell us. Laws do not explain why things behave the way they do. There is no mechanism involved in the laws. In Boyle's law, for example, we know how pressure and volume are related, but we have no explanation for why one quantity increases or decreases based on the changes in the other quantity. We only know that they increase and decrease according to the law. When we measure the forces applied to an object, the mass of the object, and the acceleration of the object, the quantities obey Newton's second law. That the quantities obey Newton's second law does not explain why the quantities obey Newton's second law. They just do.

So scientific laws simply explain how things behave. They do not result from

theories but rather are descriptions of how the physical world does what it does. Maybe it's the term *law* that makes people think scientific laws have a special place, sort of the ultimate in scientific thought. Not so. Laws are descriptions of what happens and nothing more. That doesn't mean laws are trivial, though. Laws help us develop technologies and develop theories based on the laws. Newton's laws help us figure out how to get a few people to the Moon, even if we don't know why Newton's laws work.

## Theories Explained

And with that, let's move on to theories. Theories generally provide mechanisms that explain the things we observe. There is a theory known as the *kinetic theory of gases* that provides a mechanism for understanding Boyle's law. In the kinetic theory of gases, we make various assumptions about how the molecules in a gas act. In the most basic form, we assume that gas molecules run into one another without sticking and that they move about randomly. We assume that the molecules have an average kinetic energy based on the temperature. Those basic assumptions lead to Boyle's law holding true. Because the kinetic theory of gases provides a mechanism rather than just a description of results, it qualifies as a theory. The kinetic theory of gases will never become a law, because that's not what theories become. If a theory is any good, it *explains* a law. The kinetic theory of gases explains Boyle's law, but the theory does not evolve into the law. The highest award for a theory is that it is a good theory, not that it becomes a law.

## An Educated Guess?

But what is the role of the hypothesis? For all the space spent in elementary science

---

[*] To be accurate, I have to explain that each law I have mentioned fails to hold true under certain circumstances. Within defined constraints, though, they do hold true. As long as we keep these constraints in mind, we can consider these things to be laws.

books discussing hypotheses, you would think this was a really important thing. Hypotheses are important, but maybe a bit overrated. Many books define a hypothesis as an "educated guess" that's based on an understanding of the situation. That's not complete, though. A hypothesis is an educated guess coupled with an explanation for why that guess should come true. For example, two students might guess that a puddle of water outside will disappear overnight. One student might say that this will happen because of evaporation, and the other might say this will happen because the water will soak into the concrete. A true test of these hypotheses should include a test of the explanations as well as what they observe. Now, scientists are always guessing what will happen in a given experiment, expecting certain results and explaining to themselves why they expect those results. Scientists have expectations any time they investigate the real world. If those scientists guess wrong on either what they will observe or the explanation for it, they revise their thinking or redo a procedure. But do scientists write down every hypothesis they have and report the results as part of a final report of research? Probably not, because hypotheses are simply steps that are a normal part of developing understanding of a problem. The truth about how scientists investigate things is that they mess around a whole lot, often without benefit of the statement of a formal hypothesis, and then narrow their focus. Ask someone who currently is doing research in any field of science what his or her hypothesis is, and I'm betting he or she will say, "Ummm ... Huh?" Ask that same scientist, "What problem are you working on?" and you'd better sit down and get ready for a lengthy discussion. Finally, do

hypotheses become theories? Only in the sense that they contribute to a scientist's understanding of a problem. They are part of the formation of theories, but seldom are they the central kernel from which theories grow.

To summarize, laws in science are a formal way of stating how the world behaves. Laws do not generally provide any kind of mechanism that explains why the law is true. Theories generally provide mechanisms that explain laws as well as other observations. While one might use various laws when formulating a theory, that's the extent of the connection. Theories can never become laws, because laws form the body of evidence on which we base theories. Laws can help with formulating theories, but theories do not develop into laws. Finally, hypotheses, although a natural part of the scientific process, do not generally evolve into theories. They are an important component of developing theories, but not necessarily the central component.

I'll end with an application of some of these ideas to a contentious issue, which is the ongoing battle between teaching evolution and teaching intelligent design. One of the arguments from the intelligent design crowd is that evolution is "*just* a theory." But a well-developed theory is pretty much the pinnacle of scientific achievement. The phrase "just a theory" might have significance if a theory were the precursor to something better, like maybe a law. Not so, though. The atomic theory and the theory of general relativity, to name two, are among the most solid things we know in science. Of course, I'm not putting the theory of evolution on the same level as the theory of general relativity. Too many unexplained things in the

former. Still, evolution is a pretty good working theory. And one more thing I just have to add: I have heard too many scientists claim that evolution is a fact, often in retort to the claim that it is *just* a theory. Evolution isn't a fact. Rather than claiming so, I think scientists would be better served to agree that evolution is a theory and then proceed to explain what a theory is—a coherent explanation that undergoes constant testing and often revision over a period of time. ■

# Teaching Methods

# How can hands-on science teach long-lasting understanding?

Hands-on science activities have long been touted as a great way to motivate students who otherwise might not be all that interested in science. For that matter, hands-on science activities motivate all students. Who wouldn't want to play around with cool stuff rather than read a textbook, watch a film or a teacher demonstration, or listen to the teacher pontificate?

While few people doubt that hands-on science is fun and motivating, I often hear teachers asking how they can move beyond the hands-on activities: "When exactly are students supposed to learn the science?" "Is

SCI**LINKS**.
**THE WORLD'S A CLICK AWAY**

Topic: Scientific Inquiry
Go to: *www.scilinks.org*
Code: ASQ006

"I didn't learn any more than she did ... and my junk *worked*!"

all this messing around supposed to lead, eventually, to the kids coming up with the proper concepts on their own?" The short answer to that second question is no. *Discovery learning*, in which students invent or discover the proper science concepts through hands-on experience, was once a popular notion. Unfortunately, it turns out that people left to discover concepts on their own don't discover very much. Also unfortunately, many teachers today equate inquiry learning with unsuccessful discovery learning.

## Discovery, Not!

Suppose you want students to learn the concept of systems—that is, that often we can understand a collection of objects better if we consider them as interacting parts of a whole. Some of these parts are essential to the operation of the system and some are not. As a hands-on activity you plan to have the kids investigate various systems, such as wind-up toys, battery-operated toys, flashlights, and so on.* Your fervent hope is that through these investigations, the students will come to understand a lot about systems. So you turn the kids loose on the systems. Will they discover the concepts you want them to? Probably not. They'll just play around with the systems and not necessarily pay attention to what you want them to.

Now you get smarter. You make sure some of the systems (the toys, flashlights, and so on) don't work because they're missing essential components. You also have systems that have missing or broken components but still work because the missing or broken components aren't essential. Surely now the kids will pay attention to the features you think are important.

<hr>

*Thanks to the K–1 teachers in the SALSA program in Denton, Texas, for providing the inspiration for the toy investigation.

Nah. They'll play with the ones that work and discard the ones that don't work.

## Structure the Inquiry

The solution to your dilemma? Structure the activity so the students are forced to pay attention to the features you want them to notice. Give them a task, such as answering the following questions as they play around: *Which of the objects are missing parts? Which of the objects have broken parts? If an object is missing a part, or has a broken part, does that always mean the object doesn't work? Are some parts of the objects more important than other parts? List some of these.*

By insisting that the students answer such questions, you are setting them up for the explanations you are about to provide. You can discuss systems, essential components, and nonessential components, confident that the students have had the proper experience from which to understand these concepts. All the while, the students were mostly playing around, at least according to them. In reality, the hands-on activity was purposeful because it ensured that the students gained the experience necessary to understand a few science concepts.

## Hands-On Success

Hands-on science activities motivate not just hard-to-reach students but all students. Hands-on activities just for the sake of hands-on, though, don't lead to much learning of science concepts, let alone a lasting understanding.

Structured hands-on activities in which the teacher guides and focuses the students' investigations can be an essential component in helping students develop a meaningful understanding of science concepts. Solid understanding coupled with playtime—what could be better than that? ∎

# Q: What makes for a good science fair project?

Ah, one of my pet peeves. I used to judge a lot of science fairs, but I stopped because I seldom agreed with the evaluations of the other judges. Our main point of disagreement usually centered on glitz versus substance. No doubt about it—a science fair project that *looks* impressive tends to sway the judges. Of course, I had other disagreements with other judges, so I'm glad for the opportunity to suggest what people should look for in judging science fairs, and thus what students should focus on when doing their projects. My main concerns are with the kinds of questions the project answers and the extent to which their project mimics what scientists actually do in an investigation.

## Choosing the Right Question

One way to address this issue is to name a few questions that are *not* good for science fair projects. *Why is the sky blue?*,

*Can plants survive without water?*, and *What causes volcanoes?* are examples of questions that aren't so great. The reason they're not great is that scientists already know the answers to those questions. A student doing a project inspired by such questions is simply learning a concept and reporting on it. Now, that's okay for a science classroom. It's good to learn answers to those questions and students can use inquiry to answer those questions. The purpose of a science fair, though, should be for students to address a question, the answer to which cannot be found in a textbook. Here are a few questions for which you won't find textbook answers and which might be pretty interesting for students to answer: *Does chewing gum help students do better in school? Does playing video games improve your reactions and your memory? Do people in certain-colored cars obey traffic laws better?*

These happen to be actual science fair questions I've come across over the years. The students who posed the questions had various reasons for asking the questions, but the important thing was that the students genuinely wanted to know the answers to these questions. Clearly, finding out that chewing gum helps you do better in class or discovering that playing video games is good for you are pieces of information useful for the average student. Beyond that, though, the questions lend themselves to true investigation.

## Do What Scientists Do Rather Than Follow the "Scientific Method"

In the heading for this section, the words "scientific method" are in quotes because there are disagreements as to what con-stitutes the scientific method. There is a "textbook" definition, though, that goes something like the following:

- Ask a Question
- Do Background Research
- Construct a Hypothesis
- Test Your Hypothesis by Doing an Experiment
- Analyze Your Data and Draw a Conclusion
- Communicate Your Results

Anyone who has done basic research in any scientific discipline can tell you that scientists only rarely follow this kind of structured approach. Although scientists might begin with a general question, this is followed by a whole bunch of messing around with things to become familiar with the territory. This messing around leads to refinement or even restructuring of the original question, and it might lead to a totally new question. Let me give you an example from my own research and then an example of how this might apply to a science fair project.

When I began graduate work in science education and cognitive science, I wanted to study the difference between people who understand science and people who memorize science. From my experience I knew there was a difference, but I had only primitive ideas of how to determine the difference. It took me a year and a half to get to where I knew how to conduct my research. Part of that was spent researching what others had done, part was spent simply talking to physics students, and part was spent talking to physics professors. My advisor gave me great advice in the beginning, which was to define *understanding* and *memorization* for myself before researching what others had done. That helped me keep my own perspective on the issue rather than simply parrot what other researchers thought. So I did a lot of messing around before I formulated any kind of researchable question. The bottom line was that I didn't formulate a hypothesis and then jump into my experiments.

Let's apply that to the chewing gum question. To approach this as a scientist might, one should spend a fair amount of time observing other students and talking to teachers in an effort to define what one means by "doing better in school." Do you look at test scores alone? Does attentiveness in class count? There are lots of ways to determine how well one does in school, and you have to refine things down to a specific measure of performance to get meaningful results. You also should simply observe students chewing and not chewing gum in a variety of school situations (gotta find a sympathetic teacher to allow you to do this one!). In the process, you might find behaviors related to chewing gum in class that have nothing to do with your original question. For example, you might discover that kids who chew gum in class tend to talk less. How does that relate to performance, or does it relate to performance at all?

## Controlling Variables

One of the most difficult things for students to do is figure out how to structure an investigation so as to focus on the question being asked while minimizing the effect of other factors. For chewing gum in class, you want to be able to control such contributing factors as the time of day, the day of the week, the style of the teacher, the health of the students, and the prior performance of the students. Suppose you are going to measure performance with

before and after tests. It would be a good idea to give students various kinds of tests without gum chewing involved at all, so you know something about how much students either improve or don't improve based on things other than gum chewing. In other words, you have to mess around with things again before settling on a procedure. A student who does a good job of messing around and has seriously addressed the issue of controlling variables should be commended for a job well done, even if it means not "finishing" the project with a distinct conclusion.

## Sometimes You Discover Nothing

Often scientists learn nothing from an experiment other than how to restructure the experiment. Neat, clean results are the exception rather than the rule. Yet, I have seen many science fair judges mark students down for not getting those neat, clean results. It's okay to learn nothing from an experiment other than what you did wrong because that's a common result in science. This is especially true given the relatively short amount of time students have for a science fair project. If scientists can go years without a decisive answer to a question, why expect students to get that decisive answer in a month or two?

## Judge the Process More Than the Result

Given the short amount of time students have to complete a project, given that questions that truly interest the students are likely to be complicated and difficult to define, and given that true scientific investigation seldom follows the structured steps outlined in the typical expres-

Topic: Science Fair
Go to: *www.scilinks.org*
Code: ASQ007

sion of the scientific method, it makes sense to grade students with a greater emphasis on the process of the investigation than on an eye-catching, snazzy finished product. In this way, the students gain a better understanding of scientific investigation and learn to focus on what scientists do rather than on how much Mom and Dad can help them create a cool-looking report.

I should end by saying that over the years, I have seen improvement in what schools require in a science fair project. It is more and more common to find that students are required to do an experiment rather than a report. That said, there is still too much reliance on the structured scientific method and not enough focus on, or understanding of, what scientists really do. Needless to say, the judges one uses for a science fair have at least as much influence on what the students get out of the experience as do the requirements outlined by the school. ■

# Q: How much overlap is there across science disciplines?

You often will hear that physics, chemistry, biology, and Earth science have a lot in common. In fact, many science curriculum programs stress how these disciplines are integrated and have common concepts and themes. More evidence of this integration comes from the fact that one can study and do research in biochemistry, biophysics, geophysics, and all sorts of other "cross-field" undertakings. So yes, the different disciplines can have a lot in common. On the other hand, there is a lot of specialization in science, so much so that even scientists in the same general discipline are not familiar with work that other scientists in their field are doing. For example, a physicist studying solid-state physics might have to study for months to catch up with what

I'd like to teach the world to see how science overlaps. How chemistry and Earth sciences mix with biology. They're cross-disciplines!

physicists in high-energy physics are doing, and vice versa.

Of course, the science you teach in elementary and middle school doesn't exactly match what is going on in the forefront of science, so the high degree of specialization among scientists shouldn't keep you from exploring what concepts the various scientific fields have in common. To help you with that exploration, I'm going to take a basic concept and show how it is important in four different science disciplines. Can't wait, can you? Didn't think so.

## Up and Back

Figure 1 shows a simple pendulum, which in this case is a metal washer tied to a string. If you simply hold the free end

## The motion of a pendulum relative to the equilibrium position

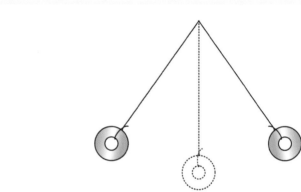

## The forces acting on a pendulum

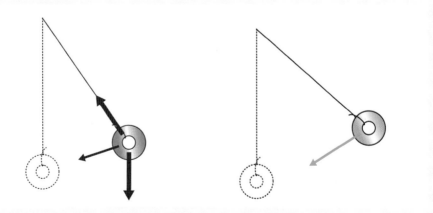

of the string, the washer is happy to stay where it is. We'll call this straight-down position the *equilibrium position.* When you pull the washer to the side and let go, the washer heads back toward the equilibrium position. It overshoots, of course, and once it overshoots and stops, it again heads back toward the equilibrium position.

What makes the washer return toward the equilibrium position is a combination of the force of gravity acting on the washer and the force the string exerts on the washer. These individual forces and the combined force are shown in Figure 2. Notice that this combined force gets larger the farther away from the equilibrium position the washer is.

Because the washer moves a lot but always tends to return to the equilibrium position, this situation is known as *dynamic equilibrium.* It is also called *stable equilib-*

*rium,* because any movement away from the equilibrium position results in a force tending to push it back to the equilibrium position. And just so you don't run out of new words to learn, this is also an example of what is called *negative feedback.* The word *negative* doesn't mean anything bad in this case, but rather refers to the fact that the force acting on the washer acts in opposition to the motion that caused it. Translation: If you push the washer in a given direction, the combined force of the gravity and the string pushes the washer opposite to that direction.

Okay, so a washer on a string is an example of a system in dynamic equilibrium that has negative feedback. The study of such pendulums comes under the subject heading of physics. Are there examples of dynamic equilibrium in other sciences? Of course! Why do you think I'm using it

## Figure 3

Graph of fox and rabbit populations over time. This graph is typical of systems in dynamic equilibrium.

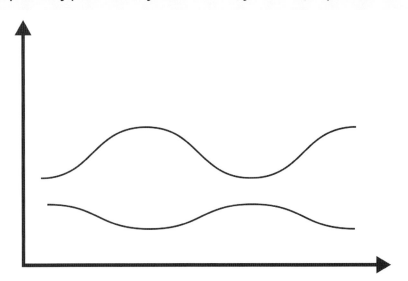

in this article? So, here's an example from another scientific discipline.

## Dinner Dynamics

In biology, predator-prey relationships are important in the study of ecosystems. For a simplified example, you can track the population of foxes and rabbits in a certain area. Foxes eat rabbits, in case you don't know. (All parent foxes tell their offspring, "Be vewy, vewy quiet, for we are hunting …") Under normal conditions, you can expect the population of foxes and rabbits to fluctuate a bit around some equilibrium positions. Now suppose you move the populations away from the equilibrium positions by, say, having a year in which an unusually large number of rabbits are born. Will the population of rabbits simply stay at the new, higher number, or is there some mechanism that will bring the population of rabbits back toward the equilibrium position?

The answer is the latter, and the mechanism that will bring the number of rabbits back toward the equilibrium position is the population of foxes. With lots more food (rabbits) available, it is likely that the birth rate of foxes will increase. More foxes means more things hunting rabbits, and the rabbit population will dwindle, moving back toward the equilibrium position. Just as with the pendulum, though, the population of rabbits will overshoot the equilibrium position (fewer rabbits than originally) because there are more foxes than before. Having overshot the equilibrium position in rabbit population, we still have a mechanism to bring the rabbits back to the equilibrium position. Fewer rabbits means fewer foxes, either through decreased birth rates or starvation or a fox exodus to look for more

plentiful food. Fewer foxes then allows the rabbit population to increase back toward the equilibrium position. Over time, you might expect a graph of the rabbit and fox population in the area to look something like Figure 3 (p. 39).

If you graphed the position of a pendulum over time, you would get a similar curve. The time scales are quite different (pendulums change position quickly and rabbit and fox populations change slowly), but the pattern is the same. All cases of dynamic equilibrium exhibit graphs similar to Figure 3 (p. 39).

## Like Clockwork

Let's move on to chemistry. Much of chemistry involves the study of chemical reactions, in which chemical A combines with chemical B to form products C and D. We can write this in general terms as $A + B \rightarrow C + D$. Often it turns out that such chemical reactions are reversible, meaning that chemical C can combine with chemical D to produce chemicals A and B. Not surprisingly, this is called a *reversible reaction*, which we write with two arrows as in $A + B \rightleftharpoons C + D$.

Now suppose that initially you have a whole bunch of chemicals A and B and hardly any C or D. You would expect, and you would be correct, that we would have a lot of A combining with B to form C and D, and not much C combining with D to form A and B. After a while, though, we end up with a lot less A and B than we started with and an accumulation of C and D. More and more C and D forming results in more and more of the reverse reaction (C and D combining to form A and B), which tends to decrease C and D and increase A and B. You can imagine that there is an equilibrium position in which the forward and reverse reactions take place at equal rates. Because of how we started, though, the chemical reaction is always overshooting the equilibrium position and then heading back toward it. The amounts of chemicals A, B, C, and D will fluctuate with time, just as the rabbits and foxes in Figure 3 (p. 39). Ta da—dynamic equilibrium. If you've ever observed a "clock reaction" in chemistry, this is an example of dynamic equilibrium.

## Carbon Feedback

Finally, how about an example of dynamic equilibrium in Earth science? There is something known as the carbonate cycle, which describes how the element carbon moves its way through various parts of the Earth. The entire carbonate cycle is a bit complicated and not completely understood, but one part of it is relatively simple. Rock formations are eroded by wind and rain in what is called *weathering* (clever name, no?). In the weathering process, carbon dioxide combines with molecules in the rock formations and is removed from the atmosphere. Now, reduced carbon dioxide in the atmosphere means less cloud cover and less rain. Less rain means less carbon dioxide removed from the atmosphere through weathering.

More carbon dioxide in the atmosphere (from whatever source) means more rain and more weathering, resulting in removal of carbon dioxide from the atmosphere. Thus, we have a feedback mechanism that sort of regulates the amount of carbon dioxide in the atmosphere. An increase in carbon dioxide in the atmosphere triggers an increase in weathering and a removal of carbon dioxide from the atmosphere. A decrease in carbon dioxide in the atmosphere triggers a decrease in weathering and less removal of carbon dioxide from the atmosphere.

## Come Together

Dynamic equilibrium is only one example of concepts that apply in different science disciplines. Energy, energy transformations, and conservation of energy are central to all sciences. Basic principles of force and motion also apply no matter what discipline you're in. Even more sophisticated concepts such as nuclear reactions are relevant to basic physics, the dating of fossils, and the function of human body systems. Despite all the compartmentalization in science, you could argue that the different science disciplines have more commonalities than they have differences. So let's all sing together, "I'd like to teach the world to sing ... how science comes together ..." ■

# Life Science

# How does the human body turn food into useful energy?

As with just about everything else involving the human body, it is absolutely amazing that we can chow down on various things and somehow use this basic action to grow, move, breathe, and all other kinds of stuff. You probably expect that the process is complicated, and it is. Pick up a textbook on biochemistry if you need to be convinced of that. On the other hand, the basic idea is pretty simple. I'm going to address the simple part in this column.

## Consider This

Suppose you want to build a cabin in a mountain valley. Unfortunately, there's an old barn sitting right where you want to build your cabin. You'll have to knock that old barn down first, right? Being a clever

You have to expend energy to get the boulder to the top of the hill.

You get a lot more energy in return as the boulder falls.

Food contains stored energy. You put energy into it (digestive processes) to get useful energy out of it.

Topic: Digestion
Go to: www.scilinks.org
Code: ASQ008

person, you look around and think that if only there was a large boulder on top of one of those surrounding hills, you could just start the boulder rolling down the hill aimed at the barn, and you would end up knocking down the barn just like that.

Well, it turns out there's just such a boulder sitting in a valley near you at a much higher elevation. The problem is that pesky hill in between. You're so fond of your plan, though, that you figure it's worth putting in a little bit of energy to get that boulder up to the top of the hill to get a lot more energy out as the boulder heads down toward the barn.

Nutrition is a whole lot like the situation with the boulder. Foods contain lots of stored chemical energy. Just as that boulder in the high valley isn't much use to you in its present position, the chemical energy stored in foods isn't, in its current state, much use for the human body. You can't smear a plate of spaghetti on your legs and expect that to help you run faster. So you put some energy into the food to get out of it the useful energy that's stored in its chemical bonds.

How do you put energy into the food? First you chew it, and then enzymes in your digestive system progressively break down the molecules in the food. Eventually you end up with sugars and fats, and finally a special molecule called adenosine triphosphate (ATP). This special molecule is the energy source your body has worked for. Individual cells in your body transform ATP into a similar molecule, adenosine diphosphate (ADP). This transformation from ATP to ADP,

the equivalent of the boulder rolling down the large hill, releases energy that the cells use for bodily functions.

A couple of clarifications. First, not all foods are sources of energy. Carbohydrates and fats are good sources of energy, but proteins, vitamins, and minerals are primarily sources of molecules that the body uses as building blocks for various processes. Second, going from the energy release from ATP to an action such as the motion of walking is still quite a complicated process. To understand this fully, you have to know how all of the human body systems work, both independently and together, and you have to know how these systems get their energy from the ATP to ADP transformation. Sorry, but there's not enough space here to go into all that.

## Take In, Take Out

There's another important energy concern with the human body, and it's the large-scale picture of how the body deals with the "balance" between the input of energy from food and the output of energy in the form of bodily functions. If you take in more food energy than your body uses (through breathing, exercise, etc.), then your body stores this excess energy as fat. If you take in less food energy than your body uses, your body relies on the fat storage for needed energy.

Clearly this balance, or lack thereof, has a lot to do with whether you gain weight, lose weight, or maintain your weight. More input energy than output energy and you gain weight. Less input energy than output energy and you lose weight. This makes a prescription for gaining or losing weight pretty simple. If you want to lose weight, eat less and exercise more.

Of course, there are specialty diets, such as the Atkins Diet, that take advantage of what we know about how the body gets energy. In that diet, you eat lots of protein and few carbohydrates and fats. Because the body gets most of its energy from carbohydrates and fats, it is forced to rely on body fat as a source of energy. Of course, that's a bit oversimplified. Your body gets more than just energy from carbohydrates, so the total effect of various diets can go beyond simple weight loss. The safe bet is the diet-exercise connection.

As you take a look at resources that describe the entire process of food energy to body energy, it's easy to get lost in all the vocabulary of the biology and the chemical reactions. If you keep in mind the big picture—putting in energy to get more out, and the balance or lack of balance between input and output—the process is a lot easier to understand. ■

# If an insect grows to human size, will it have superhuman strength?

There are lots of horror films based on small organisms such as insects growing to larger-than-human size, usually as a result of exposure to radioactive materials. It's a scary idea because an ant can lift around 20 times its own weight, and a flea can jump a flea-size tall building in a single bound. If these insects grew to gigantic proportions, couldn't they take over the world with their superstrength? The short answer is no. To understand why this is

the answer, you have to understand a bit of basic geometry and how it applies to all kinds of organisms of different sizes. We'll use an ant as an example. The legs of an ant can be modeled by a simple cylinder, as shown in the drawing. The strength of the ant's legs is proportional to the cross-sectional area of the cylinder. This is analogous to the strength of a human's legs being proportional to the cross-sectional area of the bones in the leg and the muscles in the leg.

The formula for the cross-sectional area of the cylinder (see the drawing) is $\pi r^2$, where $r$ is the radius. Let's see what happens to the cross-sectional area of this cylinder when the cylinder triples in size (the radius $r$ becomes three times as large, or $3r$). Because the radius is squared in the cross-sectional area, that means the cross-sectional area increases by a factor of $3^2$, or 9. So the cross-sectional area of an ant leg increases by a factor of 9 when the ant triples in size. That means the strength of the ant's legs increases by a factor of 9 when the ant triples in size.

Cross-sectional area of an ant's leg

We can model an ant's leg with a cylinder.

Next let's look at what happens to the *mass* of the ant when it triples in size. For this purpose, we'll make a simplification that the ant can be considered as a sphere. Now that's not a great assumption, but it will give us the same result as if we considered the ant to be made up of a collection of different geometric shapes. The mass of the ant is proportional to the *volume* of the ant, not a cross-sectional area. The volume of a sphere (the shape we're using as a model for the ant) is given by the formula $\frac{4}{3}\pi r^3$, where $r$ is the radius of the sphere. Now we're going to triple the size of the ant and see what happens to its volume. Because the formula for volume contains $r^3$, the volume increases by a factor of $3^3$, or 27, when the radius triples.

So what does this mean when an ant, or any other organism, increases in size? Because the volume of the organism increases much more rapidly than the cross-sectional area of its body parts, it means that the mass (proportional to volume) of the organism increases at a much more rapid rate than the strength (proportional to cross-sectional area) of the organism.

## Strength Versus Mass

Let's apply our knowledge to a really big increase in the size of an ant or other

As an ant increases in size, the cross-sectional area of its leg, and hence its strength, increases by a factor of 9.

We can model an ant's body with a sphere.

As an ant increases in size, the volume of the ant, and hence its mass, increases by a factor of 27.

organism. The strength of an organism is related to the cross-sectional area of its muscles and the cross-sectional area of its bones or other skeletal structures. The mass and weight of an organism are related to its volume. So imagine that an ant increases in size by a factor of, say, 50. The cross-sectional area of the ant's legs, which determines its strength, increases by a factor of 2,500. The volume of the ant, which determines its mass, increases by a factor of 125,000! The ant gets a lot heavier, but the increase in strength doesn't keep up with the increase in mass. As a result, the ant's legs might not even be able to support its weight. At best, the ant will be about as strong as a human of the same size. That flea that could jump tall flea buildings in a single bound could, if increased to human size, jump a fence at best.

This relationship between strength and cross-sectional area, and mass and volume, explains why an elephant is not put together like an ant or a flea or a spider. An elephant has really thick legs, because it needs that extra cross-sectional area strength to support its large mass. Hippos and rhinos have those same large legs to support their weight. A giraffe's legs are rather thin and spindly, but the giraffe's body isn't nearly as big as that of an elephant, rhino, or hippo.

## Gaining and Losing Heat

There's another important consideration when organisms change scale, or increase in size. As an organism increases in size, its metabolic requirements (energy use) increase according to an increase in volume. That's because the number of cells in an organism's body, which require energy, is proportional to the organism's volume.

You might think, then, that the metabolism of an organism should increase according to an increase in volume. Greater volume means more cells that require energy, which means a corresponding increase in metabolism to feed those extra cells.

There's a good reason this doesn't happen, and it has to do with how an organism gains or loses body heat. The rate at which an organism does this depends on the *surface area* of the organism. To understand what happens to an organism's surface area when it increases in size, we have to go back to modeling the organism as a sphere.

The surface area of a sphere depends on the *square* of the radius (the formula for the surface area of a sphere is $4\pi r^2$, where $r$ is the radius of the sphere). The sphere's volume depends on the *cube* of the radius. As we saw earlier, when the radius increases, the cube of the radius increases much more rapidly than the square of the radius. That means that the volume of our sphere (and hence our organism) increases much more rapidly than does its surface area.

In other words, an organism's ability to gain and lose heat doesn't keep up with its metabolic requirements as it grows in size. If a mouse grew to the size of an elephant and its metabolism kept up with the change in volume, the mouse would literally burn up because it couldn't dissipate heat fast enough.

The solution to this would seem to be obvious. As organisms get larger, you might expect that their metabolism increases in the same mathematical way as their surface area. Turns out that's not quite the case. Their metabolism actually increases more rapidly than their surface area (no profound reason for this—it's just the way things seem to be). If this is the case, then why don't large animals burn up from their metabolism? The answer is that larger animals have features that help them dissipate and gain heat faster than you might normally expect. Elephants are a great example. They have those big floppy ears, filled with blood vessels, that they use for cooling and heating.

## Looks Can Be Deceiving

Let's summarize by admitting that we have no examples of organisms dramatically decreasing or increasing in size, except in comic books or movies. To figure out what *might* happen, we use what we know about geometry, size, strength, and metabolism. We also look at separate organisms that are already on different scales. It does seem clear, though, that nature takes care of potential inequities should an organism end up much smaller or much larger than it currently is. Reassuring, huh? ■

# How does photosynthesis work?

Energy transformations are an important part of the functioning of ecosystems, and a key part of those energy transformations is photosynthesis. *Photosynthesis* is the process by which plants, bacteria, and other organisms use the energy of sunlight to manufacture food in the form of sugar. If it weren't for photosynthesis, the energy source (sunlight) for all ecosystems would be useless. In other words, we'd all die, even though we might have really nice tans. In "How does the human body turn food into useful energy?" I discussed how humans use food for energy, so it only makes sense that we should address how we get that food in the first place, via photosynthesis. In doing so, I'll stick with photosynthesis as it occurs in green plants. In addition to providing food for animals that eat plants and for the plants themselves, photosynthesis provides another valuable service. The process removes carbon dioxide from the air (a waste product for animals) and replaces it with oxygen, something animals need to survive.

Using an extremely complicated, patented process called Photosynthesis, we've combined energy, water, carbon dioxide, and other chemicals to create **High Energy Sugars!** It's guaranteed to make plants grow. Some side effects such as oxygen and sap have been reported. But that's natural.

## A Simple Process?

You can represent the overall process of photosynthesis in a simple way. Plants take in carbon dioxide and water and produce glucose (a sugar) and oxygen.

As a chemical equation, this looks like the following:

$$\text{carbon dioxide} + \text{oxygen} \xrightarrow{\text{produces}} \text{glucose} + \text{water}$$

### Figure 1

## Sometimes you have to expend energy to get energy.

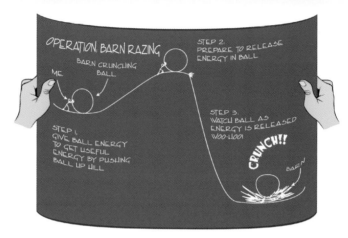

### Figure 2

## Energy transfers in photosynthesis

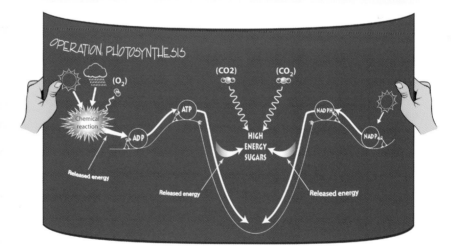

or

$$6CO_2 + 6H_2O \xrightarrow[produces]{} C_6H_{12}O_6 + 6O_2$$

The numbers refer to how many molecules of each type take part in the reaction and how many atoms of each type (carbon, hydrogen, and oxygen) are in each molecule. Anyway, this looks like a simple procedure. Carbon dioxide is available in the atmosphere, and plants are good at absorbing water, so why can't plants (or any other organisms, for that matter) just combine carbon dioxide and water to produce glucose and oxygen? For the answer to that, simply look at your nearest bottle of sparkling water. It contains lots of water and lots of dissolved carbon dioxide, but you won't notice the spontaneous generation of sugar and oxygen in that sparkling water. Obviously, just bringing the proper ingredients together doesn't produce the desired result. So although the overall process of photosynthesis might look simple, the details must not be simple.

## Examining the Details

If you head to the internet or your favorite textbook to learn about the details of photosynthesis, you will likely find that the vocabulary becomes overwhelming in a hurry. In fact, you can soon see nothing but the vocabulary words and become confused in short order. One reason for this is that photosynthesis is quite complicated, and the other is that many biology references are overly fond of vocabulary. To avoid this problem, I'm going to stick to the basics of photosynthesis and focus primarily on the energy transformations involved. In fact, I'm going to begin by recalling a basic energy concept that I've addressed in other columns. After the energy discussion, I'll talk briefly about the plant structures involved in photosynthesis. First, though, the energy.

If you have a ball sitting at the top of a hill, all it takes is a little nudge for the ball to roll down the hill, enabling you to use its energy for some useful or not-so-useful purpose. If that ball is not at the top of a hill, though, you might have to first give the ball some energy before you can get energy out of it (see Figure 1).

Relating this concept to plants, a plant uses two high-energy molecules to create sugars. Those molecules are adenosine triphosphate (ATP) and "reduced" nicotinamid adenosine dinucleotide phosphate (NADPH). You

### Figure 3

## Photosynthesis occurs in sacs called thylakoids inside chloroplasts.

Thylakoids

can think of these two molecules as balls at the top of their respective hills—they are poised to provide the energy needed to create sugar out of carbon dioxide. The problem is that plants don't just have these molecules sitting around (although they do have the chemicals necessary to produce the high-energy molecules). Enter light. In a complex process, plants use light energy to transform a couple of low-energy molecules—adenosine diphosphate (ADP) and nicotinamid adenosine dinucleotide phosphate (NADP)—into the high-energy molecules they need. Figure 2 (p. 54) shows the transfers of energy involved in this process.

What's interesting is that the difference between the low-energy molecules and the high-energy molecules is relatively small. ATP has one more phosphate group (a phosphorous atom plus four oxygen atoms, with a couple of extra electrons) than ADP, and NADPH is the same as NADP, with the exception of one additional hydrogen atom that's missing an electron. These differences in energy are a result of the different numbers of electrons and their positions in relation to the atoms. This is common in chemistry. Simply changing how close an electron is to the nucleus of an atom changes the total energy of an atom, just as changing the distance a ball is from the surface of the Earth changes the energy of the situation. Of course, these tiny energy differences add up to a considerable amount, because we're dealing with millions of ATP and NADPH molecules.

I should end by saying that you will run across the molecules ADP, ATP, NADP, and NADPH in lots of chemical reactions that take place in living organisms. As with photosynthesis, following the energy transformations will help you understand the overall processes in those reactions.

## The Plant Factory

As I said, the complete process of photosynthesis is pretty darned complicated. There are lots of plant parts involved, lots of different molecules involved, and many chemical pathways. If you keep the overall energy transfer in mind, though, you should have an easier time wading through a more complex explanation. Here is a brief overview of how and where photosynthesis occurs.

## Using Light

Plants have a pigment called *chlorophyll* that absorbs light in the red-orange and blue-violet parts of the spectrum. Chlorophyll reflects green light, which is why plants are green. Parts of the chlorophyll known as *antennae* absorb the light energy and funnel the light energy to what are called *reaction centers*, where another energy transfer takes place by the movement of electrons from molecule to molecule. Plants that thrive without a lot of sunlight have a larger number of antenna sites to gather enough light for photosynthesis under such conditions.

The main chemical reactions of photosynthesis take place in plant structures called *chloroplasts*, and specifically in something called the *thylakoids*. Thylakoids are flat sacs that contain the chemicals such as NADP and ADP that are necessary for photosynthesis to occur (Figure 3, p. 55).

## Gases In, Gases Out

Plants don't breathe the way humans do, and gases don't pass easily through the waxy parts of leaves, but leaves have special sites known as *stomata* that can open and close. Carbon dioxide enters through the stomata, and oxygen leaves (no pun intended) in the reverse direction. Plants lose lots of water in this process, so the ability to gather lots of water is a good thing for plants. Special tubes known as *xylem* transport water efficiently from the roots of a plant to the leaves.

## Photosynthetic Products

Plants use the sugar products of photo-synthesis to produce carbohydrates. These carbohydrates are converted to useful energy that plants use to grow and reproduce, and they also serve as the main food source that animals use for all bodily functions. I should also end by giving thanks to our friends the plants, without which we'd starve and run out of oxygen. Thanks, plants. ■

Topic: Photosynthesis
Go to: *www.scilinks.org*
Code: ASQ009

## Resource

Robertson, B. 2006. How does the human body turn food into useful energy? *Science and Children* 43 (6): 60–61.

# Q: How do animals navigate during migration?

Migrating animals do amazing things. Homing pigeons can find their way "home" across hundreds of miles; salmon return to their spawning location thousands of miles away; turtles travel more than eight thousand miles to lay their eggs in the spot where they originally hatched; Sassy, Chance, and Shadow found their way home across miles of wilderness (obscure movie reference); and my son unerringly finds his way to the kitchen in the middle of the night when it's pitch black.

Scientists have studied how animals navigate around the globe (my son excluded) and discovered a number of mechanisms. Some animals, including

"I appreciate you asking for directions. But how reliable is 'Just follow your nose!' from a toucan?"

birds and whales, use landmarks, the position of the Sun in the sky, and even the position of stars. Salmon appear to rely almost exclusively on their sense of smell to return them to their spawning grounds. One of the most remarkable methods, though, depends on the Earth's magnetic field, which is what I'm going to address in this column.

## Magnetism

To see how magnets are involved in navigation, get two bar magnets. Tie a string around the middle of one of the magnets, and hang it so it can swing freely (Figure 1).

Now bring the second bar magnet near the first one. Move the second one around and you'll

Figure 1

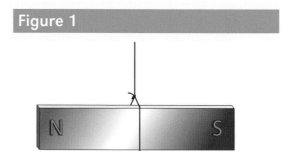

Figure 2

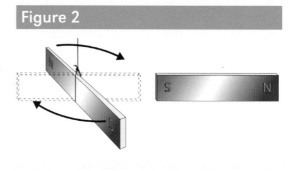

Figure 3

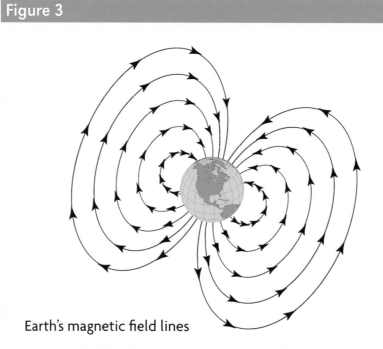

Earth's magnetic field lines

notice that the magnet on the string moves in response. It's as if the magnet on the string is "lining up" with the magnet in your hand (Figure 2).

Now find yourself some iron filings. You can get these from a science supply company or simply collect your own: Wrap one of your magnets in a plastic bag and drag the wrapped magnet through any old pile of loose dirt or sand. A whole bunch of iron filings should collect on the outside of the bag. Once you've collected the iron filings, hold the plastic-wrapped magnet over a sheet of paper and remove the magnet from the plastic. The iron filings should fall onto the sheet of paper. Next, move your magnet slowly around on the underside of the paper with the filings and notice that the iron filings move around in response to the movement of the magnet.

The lesson we're supposed to learn from this little activity is that magnets tend to line up with other magnets, and certain materials that contain iron (such as iron filings) tend to line up with magnets. What does this have to do with animal navigation, you ask? Well, it turns out that the Earth itself is a very large magnet.

You have undoubtedly seen drawings of "magnetic field lines" that are generated by the Earth (see Figure 3). These magnetic field lines indicate how a magnet or an iron-containing substance will orient itself when immersed in the magnetic field of the Earth. Because the direction of the Earth's magnetic field is different at different locations on the Earth, one can tell exactly where one is on Earth by detecting the direction of the Earth's magnetic field at any position on the Earth. An ordinary compass is just a magnet that orients itself with the Earth's magnetic field lines, indicating which direction is north. Because the Earth's magnetic field also is oriented at different angles toward or away from the surface of the Earth and also has different strengths at different locations, a good magnet can also tell you what latitude you're at on Earth's surface.

## Built-In Compasses

Now, wouldn't it be convenient if migratory animals simply carried compasses with them so they could find their way around Earth? That turns out to be pretty close to what happens. Many animals are born with a substance called *magnetite*, which acts like iron filings. The magnetite in their bodies, usually located in a particular part of the brain or near nasal cavities (birds have it in their beaks), lines up with the Earth's magnetic field and lets the animals know when they're on or off course. In a sense, these animals have their own built-in GPS system that tells them when they're on or off course according to the Earth's magnetic field. How do we know that animals use magnetic effects to navigate? Pretty simple. If you place baby loggerhead turtles in a tank of water, they take off swimming. If you alter the magnetic field that surrounds the tank of water, the turtles start swimming in different directions. In fact, the direction the turtles swim corresponds to the direction they should swim at different parts of the Earth to reach their spawning grounds. Whales also alter their migration routes when people artificially alter the normal magnetic field for their particular location.

Homing pigeons rely heavily on orienting the magnetite in their beaks with the Earth's magnetic field to find their way back to where they started. We know this because major disruptions in the Earth's magnetic field throw homing pigeons

Topic: Earth's Magnetic Field
Go to: *www.scilinks.org*
Code: ASQ010

all out of whack. Giant solar flares on the Sun (associated with sunspots) distort the Earth's magnetic field significantly for the duration of the flares, and pigeons trying to line themselves up with that distorted field get lost. Organizations devoted to flying homing pigeons for sport regularly contact the National Oceanic and Atmospheric Association to get reports on solar activity, checking to see if it's safe to fly their homing pigeons.

## Sense of Direction?

Finally, magnets and navigation can shed light on the age-old question of why males tend not to stop and ask for directions. There is a tendency for human males to rely on geographic methods for orienting themselves and getting from one place to another. Females tend to rely more on landmarks such as street names and buildings. Well, it turns out that most males have a higher concentration than females of iron-filing-like materials in their nasal passages, materials that can line up with the Earth's magnetic field. Seems natural, then, that males will rely on this magnetic navigation more so than on landmark navigation—they're just using the iron filings they were born with. (No, I'm not making this up!) Of course, that doesn't make males infallible in their navigational abilities, so you women can feel free to continue to yell at your spouses for ending up 300 miles out of your way. ■

# Q: How do animals communicate underwater?

Well, they often use hand signals, such as the "OK" sign, and sometimes they write on message boards. So much for how SCUBA divers (classified as animals) communicate! Other than my knowledge of sound waves and how they move through air and water, along with the fact that whales and dolphins make cool sounds, SCUBA (Some Come Up Barely Alive) diver communication was about the extent of my understanding of this question prior to trying to answer it. So I did a bit of research. I discovered lots of interesting things, so I'll share them.

## Sights and Smells

Before beginning, I want to expand the definition of communication to include ways of finding out about our surroundings. That means that you don't need two

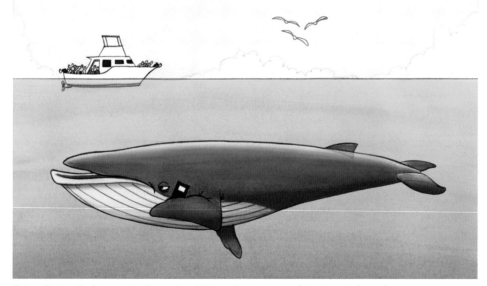

"Hey, listen, Bob, can I call you back? Another group of tourists is here."

Figure 1

## Sound moving along a wall

animals to have communication, although much of what I discuss will concern two or more animals at a time. That said, let's start with communicating using sight. Aside from the obvious, such as seeing where a reef is or where the water surface is, underwater creatures use their sight to communicate lots of things. Fish and sea-dwelling mammals have distinctive markings, shapes, and sizes. They use these clues to figure out what other swimming things might be food or might be looking at *them* as food. Colors and markings also let the fish and mammals know who's male and who's female, an important distinction for propagation of the species. Various swimming motions also play a part in sight communication, from predator-prey to courtship. And who hasn't seen

a photo or video of crustaceans such as crabs and lobsters waving those pincers to defend territory?

Smell plays another big part in underwater communication. Fish, like their human counterparts, emit and can detect *pheromones* that facilitate mating procedures. (Yep, humans use pheromones too.) If you've ever dropped food in one part of an aquarium and watched fish move quickly to where the food is, you know that fish also use smell to locate food. Crustaceans and sea mammals do the same. You probably already know that salmon travel many miles to spawn at their birthplace. To our best knowledge, those salmon use smells to guide them all those miles. Truly remarkable, as I can't imagine smelling my way to my birthplace in Northern

California. Maps work. Dolphins might also benefit from maps, as they have no sense of smell, period. For the record, most land-based mammals have limited to non-existent ability to smell underwater.

## Sounds and Water

The most interesting form of underwater animal communication involves sound waves. Before I talk about that, I have a few things for you to do. Grab a friend and a hammer (or other hard object) and find a long outside wall or chain-link fence. Give your friend the hammer and station yourself at least 150 feet (along the wall or fence) from your friend. Watch and listen as your friend strikes the wall or fence with the hammer. Notice when you see the hit and when you hear it. Repeat this, but hold your ear up to the fence or wall as your friend hits it with the hammer. Notice when you see the hit and when you hear it. Also notice how loud this sound is compared with the sound you hear without your ear up to the wall or fence (Figure 1).

For your next task, take your friend to a swimming pool or to the nearest bathtub. (Needless to say, wear a swimsuit in both cases, unless your friend is a really close friend.) Take with you a couple of solid objects to bang together. Have your friend bang the objects together underwater while you are above water. Hear anything? Then repeat while your head is underwater. While you're listening, close your eyes and see if you can tell where the sound is coming from. Finally, keep your head underwater while your friend bangs the objects together above water. Hear anything?

I had you do those things (and I hope you actually did them) so you could experience, rather than just read about, what I'm about to explain about sound waves in

and out of water. Without your ear up to the wall or fence, you should have noticed a significant difference between when you saw your friend hit the wall or fence and when you heard the sound. No big surprise, as you hear thunder long after you see lightning. (If they occur at the same time, that's really bad.) With your ear against the wall or fence, however, the sight of the hit and the sound occurred almost simultaneously, yes? This means that sound travels through solids much faster than sound travels through air. Now, water isn't exactly a solid, but like a solid, it's a lot denser than air. As a result, sound travels through water almost five times faster than it does air. Turns out that, at least for low frequencies (low sound pitches), sound also doesn't dissipate as fast in water as in air. You experienced this if you listened to sounds made underwater while your head was underwater. Loud, wasn't it? At that same time, you no doubt had trouble figuring out where the sound was coming from. That's due more to human hearing than it is to the nature of sound in water. Animals that live underwater apparently have little trouble distinguishing where sounds come from. Finally, you probably found it almost impossible to hear sounds made underwater when you were out of the water, with the same result for sounds made out of water while you were underwater. This is because the air-water surface is almost a perfect reflector for sound waves—sound doesn't travel well, if at all, from water to air and from air to water. So if you want an animal that's underwater to hear you, you have to *make* the sound underwater.

## Communication Methods

Maybe the best known underwater communication occurs among whales and

Topic: Sonar
Go to: www.scilinks.org
Code: ASQ011

dolphins. Because we don't speak whale or dolphin, we really can only infer what they're communicating. Although we can't know for sure, it does appear that whales and dolphins use sound to attract mates, to repel rivals, to communicate within and between social groups, and to find food. Not surprisingly, these sounds are relatively low frequencies—the ones that travel farthest underwater.

With respect to finding food, these animals use what's known as *echolocation*, which is what bats use in the air to locate food. The mechanism for echolocation is pretty simple. The animal emits a sound and then listens for echoes (sound reflections) that bounce off various things, including potential food. How long it takes for the echo to return tells the animal how far away the reflecting object is, where it is, and even in which direction and at what speed the object is moving. That last bit of information requires the ability to detect differences in pitch between the emitted sound and reflected sound, because sound reflected off moving objects shifts in frequency (this is known as the Doppler effect). And yes, the police use a similar system (using electromagnetic waves rather than sound) to determine how much money to charge you based on how much you exceed the posted speed limit.

Of course, whales and dolphins aren't the only animals that use sound to communicate underwater. So-called "snapping shrimp" click an oversize claw together and make a really loud sound that actually stuns their prey. Sea lions and harp seals also send out sounds to others of their species. Harp seals are pretty interesting in that they vary the frequency (pitch) of their sounds and insert pauses so as not to "talk over" one another. Damselfish emit a series of "pops" to defend their territory, and many other fish use teeth grinding, muscle flexing, and swim bladder vibrating to produce sounds associated with mating and with territorial concerns.

A surprising underwater communicator is the hippopotamus. A Massachusetts scientist observed hippos making loud sounds while above water, resulting in hippos in other parts of the river surfacing. Besides the confusion resulting from hippos being in Massachusetts (not really), one might wonder how a sound made above water could be heard underwater (remember—the air-water surface is almost a perfect sound reflector). Turns out that while making that above-water sound, hippos simultaneously use a big blob of blubber underneath the jaw to emit a loud noise. This blubber is submerged, so it's the source of sound that travels underwater. Even more amazing is that hippos, with ears similar to human ears, can hear these underwater sounds and know where they came from. The speculation is that hippos actually use their jaws to sense the underwater sound vibrations. And since sound travels so much farther underwater than in air, hippos can communicate with one another for long distances up and down a river.

## SONAR and Such

I started this column with human communication underwater, so I guess I'll end with it. Humans create many sounds underwater, some purposeful and some inadvertent. Among the purposeful is the human version of echolocation, called

SONAR (Sound Orientation Navigation And Ranging). Basically, things such as submarines emit sounds and record the echoes, thus figuring out where other subs or hard things such as icebergs are, whether or not they're moving, and how fast and in what direction they're moving. Here, as with hippos, it's a good thing that sound waves travel much farther and faster in water than in air. Among the inadvertent sounds people make are the sounds from ships, oil rigs, and other underwater machinery. The inadvertent sounds have led to the concern that human sounds might be interfering with the communication of other animals. No solid evidence of that yet, but it's worth studying.

Many years ago, people used to think of the oceans as "silent." No doubt that was due to the fact that sounds don't travel well from water to air (it gets reflected). Now we know better, and we might want to consider the sounds we make underwater. ■

# Q: Do plants communicate?

Oh yes. Sometimes their conversation is flowery, sometimes not. Plants with problems try to converse and get to the root of the problem, but if not, they have been known to stalk one another. This often creates a situation where one plant leaves town, reputation soiled. But seriously, folks ...

"Bee-Four-One-Niner, you're clear to land."

Plants do communicate with other plants and organisms as well as with insects, though it's unlikely they use lame puns about plant parts. In this column, I'll discuss this communication with separate categories: communication within a plant, communication between plants, communication between plants and insects, and communication between plants and insects together. This final category involves results that are simply amazing, but I'll save that for last. First is the communication within a plant.

## Within the Plant

You probably know that plants draw nutrients and fluids in through their roots and then transport those things to the rest of the plant. How leaves interact with the atmosphere affects the internal pressure of the plant and thus affects the transportation of materials from the roots to the rest of the plant. And of course, the interaction of leaves with the Sun provides food for the rest of the plant through photosynthesis. The communication goes further than that, though. Plants, like humans, use long chain molecules called *ribonucleic acid* (RNA) to send messages. These messages are sent within cells in humans and both within cells and from one cell to another in plants. In fact, the more accurate name for this molecule is *messenger RNA*. Messenger RNA travels in both directions (from leaves to roots and from roots to leaves and flowers) and affects levels of proteins in different parts of the plant. These protein levels can convey information such as the overall physical condition of the plant, the presence of various types of invaders (such as bacteria or viruses or Zim), and even what season it is. So plants have sort of a chemical phone network within themselves.

## Plant to Plant

Plants also communicate with the outside world in several ways. One way is through the roots. The roots of a plant release chemicals that can either attract or repel other organisms (either competing plants or invading insect pests). Sometimes this is beneficial to the plant, but sometimes not. For example, there are certain kinds of parasitic plants (plants that live off other plants with or without giving a benefit to the "host" plant) that require the presence of particular chemicals. The key here is that the necessary chemicals come from the host plant. So the seeds of a parasitic plant hang around in the soil until they encounter chemicals emitted by the roots belonging to a potential host plant. Then the parasite germinates and grows and latches onto the host plant.

Another way plants communicate with other plants is through chemicals released into the air. The following cool thing happened with wild tobacco plants and sagebrush. Scientists investigated an area that contained both kinds of plants (Karban and Baxter 2001). They clipped the leaves of some of the sagebrush plants in a way that mimicked damage caused by insects. This caused the sagebrush to release a chemical (methyl jasmonate). The tobacco plants downwind from the damaged sagebrush then increased their production of a different chemical (known as PPO) that made them less tasty to insects. These tobacco plants then sustained 60% less damage from grasshoppers than tobacco plants not near the sagebrush—clearly an interplant warning system!

## Plant to Insect

Plants can communicate with insects as well as with other plants. One way is visually. In case you didn't know, many plants require insects to reproduce. It's the old birds and bees thing. Insects (and some birds and bats) go after the pollen and nectar in flowers because, well, they use them. The side effect here is that as insects travel from plant to plant, the pollen they carry on their bodies is deposited on the stigma of the next plant, resulting in cross-pollination. (Find a good primer on pollination at *www.mbgnet.net/bioplants/pollination.html.*)

So it's a good thing for both bees (and other insects, too) and plants for the bees to be able find the nectar and pollen easily. Enter the visual communication. Bees and other insects have eyes that are sensitive to ultraviolet light, and it turns out that many flowers show a pattern in ultraviolet light that is not visible to humans. The patterns vary from flower to flower, but they have one thing in common, which is that the patterns all guide insects to where they need to go. Some ultraviolet patterns simply highlight the pollen centers, while others create a "bull's-eye" pattern or even a "landing strip" pattern that directs insects to the pollen. For cool photos of these patterns, check out *www.naturfotograf.com/UV_flowers_list.html.*

## Amazing Plants

Now we get to the really amazing stuff. There have been a number of studies involving both plant-to-plant and plant-to-insect communication. Scientists in Japan subjected lima bean plants to spider mites that eat up the lima bean plants (Shimoda and Takabayashi 2001). When the mites attacked the plants, the plants produced a chemical that made them taste bad to the mites, just as the tobacco plants did in the previous study.

Like the sagebrush in that previous study, the lima bean plants also produced other chemicals that traveled through the air to the other lima bean plants, causing the other lima bean plants to produce the bad-tasting chemical. Now for the kicker: Some of the chemicals released by the attacked lima bean plants attracted *other* mites—mites that ate the original spider mites! So in addition to using a plant's early warning system, the lima beans were able to call in the "Air Force." And this ability to call in air support is not limited to lima beans. Corn plants apparently can use chemicals to attract wasps that help destroy worms that are attacking the corn (Turlings, Tumlinson, and Lewis 1990). Other examples exist, so this is apparently a common form of communication between plants themselves and between plants and insects.

I suppose I shouldn't end this chapter without addressing communication between plants and humans. I recall that a number of years ago it was quite fashionable to talk or sing to houseplants on the theory that this improved the health and growth rate of the plants. Although there appears to be some evidence for this kind of positive interaction between human singing and plant health, a lot of what is written on the subject is tied to some pretty flaky stuff. I even ran across one setup where a canary in one city was wired for sound and this sound was electrically connected to a plant in another city. (I'm not sure why separate cities were necessary!) Supposedly, the plant responded in various ways to the canary's voice and even sent messages back to the canary (Kac 1994). The whole thing might have been legitimate, but color me skeptical—in ultraviolet shades, please. ∎

## References

Kac, E. 1994. Essay concerning human understanding. *www.ekac.org/Essay.html.*

Karban, R., and K. J. Baxter. 2001. Induced resistance in wild tobacco with clipped sagebrush neighbors: The role of herbivore behavior. *Journal of Insect Behavior* 14 (2): 147–156.

Shimoda, T., and J. Takabayashi. 2001. Response of Oligota kashmirica benefica, a specialist insect predator of spider mites, to volatiles from prey-infested leaves under both laboratory and field conditions. *Entomologia Experimentalis et Applicata* 101 (1): 41–47.

Turlings, T. C. J., J. H. Tumlinson, and W. J. Lewis. 1990. Exploitation of herbivore-induced plant odors by host-seeking parasitic wasps. *Science* 250 (4985): 1251–1253.

# Earth and Space Science

# Q: What causes lightning and thunder?

The mechanism that leads to lightning is complicated and not well understood. That it's not well understood isn't surprising, as this is often the case when going from scientific models to the real world. Even so, we can paint a reasonable picture of what happens if we understand a few basics about static electricity.

There are two kinds of charges in the world—positive and negative. Our model of the atom includes positively charged nuclei surrounded by negatively charged electrons. The effects of static electricity are *usually* a result of electrons moving from one place to another, leading to an arrangement of charges in which positive and negative charges are concentrated in certain areas. With these concentrations,

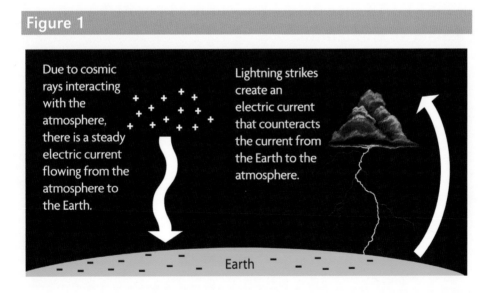

**Figure 1**

Due to cosmic rays interacting with the atmosphere, there is a steady electric current flowing from the atmosphere to the Earth.

Lightning strikes create an electric current that counteracts the current from the Earth to the atmosphere.

Earth

the microscopic forces between individual charges result in large-scale, observable forces between objects.

For example, when you rub a balloon on your hair, negatively charged electrons leave your hair and join the molecules on the surface of the balloon, leaving behind a net positive charge on your hair. Because opposite charges attract, there is now an attraction between the negatively charged balloon and your positively charged hair. Just as a balloon can pick up electrons from your hair, your body can pick up excess electrons when you rub your feet on a carpet. Then when you get near a metal object, which readily conducts electrons, you get a shock. Why? Because *electric forces*—the naturally occurring attraction between unlike charges or the repulsion between like charges—between the excess electrons on your finger and the concentrated positive charge on the metal object *ionize* the

air. *Ionization* is the process of creating positive and negative particles that are able to conduct an *electric current*, or the motion of charges. So, the ionized air is a path along which an electric current can move.

This brings us to a major idea when dealing with electric charges. Because elec-

Figure 2

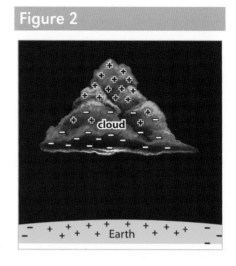

## Figure 3

The large negative charge at the bottom of the cloud means Earth just below the cloud is positive with respect to the cloud.

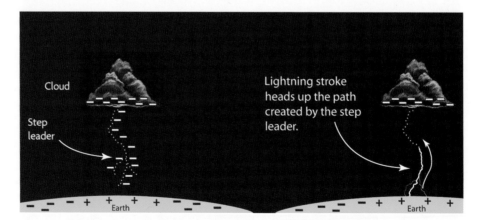

tric forces are quite strong and far-reaching, objects in the universe tend to be electrically neutral (equal numbers of positive and negative charges). The equal numbers result because any major buildup of charges (due to any number of interactions between objects) leads to large electric forces. This results in electric currents, which tend to equalize the charge distribution. In other words, large concentrations of either positive or negative charges don't last long because electric currents, resulting from electric forces, tend to equalize the distribution.

## Charge Separation on Earth

It might surprise you that there is a more-or-less constant charge separation between the Earth and the atmosphere, no matter what the weather. The Earth is negatively charged, and there is a gradual move toward a more positive charge as you move up in the atmosphere.

Scientists believe that *cosmic rays* (subatomic particles traveling the universe) are largely responsible for creating this charge separation between the Earth and the atmosphere; they ionize molecules in the atmosphere through collisions.

Well, if everything in the universe tends toward electric neutrality, why then don't electrons move around until the atmosphere "discharges" itself? Turns out they do. Scientists have measured the rate of this discharge, and if this discharge were the only motion of charges in the atmosphere, the Earth and the atmosphere would neutralize each other in a very short time.

Of course, I already told you that the charge separation between the Earth and the atmosphere is more-or-less constant. This means that there must be something that keeps "charging up" this system and maintaining the initial charge separa-

tion. That something is lightning, which acts like a battery keeping the Earth-atmosphere system charged up. There are about 100,000 lightning strikes per second on Earth—a sufficient number to maintain a charge separation between the atmosphere and the Earth. Figure 1 (p. 75) explains how that happens.

## So What Causes Lightning Already?

To fully understand what causes lightning, you need to understand what goes on in a thunderstorm. A thunderstorm consists of a number of *convection* cells, which are circulations of rising and sinking air. Along with the rising and sinking air are sinking water droplets and/or ice particles. As the water droplets and ice particles sink inside these convection cells, they cause an overall charge separation in the thunderclouds. There are competing theories as to how this charge separation happens, but the result is well documented. The clouds end up with an overall negative charge at the bottom, an overall positive charge at the top, and a concentration of positive charges toward the center. The negative charge buildup at the bottom of the cloud is much more concentrated than the normal negative charge of the Earth, so the bottom of the cloud is more negative than the Earth. Because electric forces get stronger the closer things are, the electric forces between the bottom of the cloud and the Earth are very strong—much stronger than the electric forces between the Earth and the positive charges in the upper part of the cloud. It looks something like Figure 2.

This charge separation between the bottom of the cloud and the Earth ionizes the air between the cloud and the Earth and does so in steps. Something called a

*step leader*, which is nothing more than ionized air, begins to stretch from the cloud to the Earth. It progresses in steps of about 50 meters (hence the name *step* leader) and brings excess negative charges from the cloud toward the Earth.

This step leader paves the way for an electric current because it's a path of ionized particles that are primed to conduct an electric current. This is just like what happens when you get near a metal object after shuffling your feet on a carpet. When this step leader reaches the Earth, or often just before it does, a large electrical current emerges from the Earth and follows the path the step leader created. The step leader itself consists of moving charges and constitutes a small electric current, but the return electric current from the Earth is much larger and, thus, the current we associate with the major lightning flash. So, lightning actually moves from the Earth upward.

The initial discharge is followed by more buildup of charge by the same mechanism (sinking water or ice droplets) that caused the charge buildup in the cloud to begin with. This is followed by more discharges that also follow along the path created by the step leader. These multiple discharges are what we see as lightning. The fact that there are many such discharges from the Earth up the path created by the step leader accounts for the repeated flashing you see in a lightning stroke. Needless to say, this whole thing happens very quickly (Figure 3, p. 76).

Sometimes the step leader comes across a pocket of positive charge in the atmosphere (created by those cosmic rays), and the lightning strike occurs without ever hitting the ground. Other concentra-tions of positive charge in the atmosphere can even cause horizontal lightning.

To revisit where we started, note that each lightning bolt results in negative charges flowing to the Earth (because the bottom layer of the cloud is more negative than the Earth). This maintains that constant charge separation between the Earth and the atmosphere that I discussed earlier.

## Sounds of Lightning

Once you know what lightning is, thunder is pretty simple. A lightning bolt creates incredibly intense heat. A lightning bolt is actually hotter than the surface of the Sun! This intense heat causes a rapid expansion and then contraction of the air around the lightning. The rapid expansion and contraction creates sound waves, which are nothing more than air molecules moving back and forth. The vibration of molecules (sound!) spreads out in all directions, producing thunder. Now, because sound travels much slower than light, you hear the thunder after you see the lightning. Sound travels about one mile in five seconds, so if you count the seconds between the lightning flash and the thunderclap, you can figure out how far away the lightning is. Just divide the time by five, and that's the number of miles away the lightning is (for example, if you count to 20, the lightning is 20/5, or 4 miles away).

## More About Lightning

Here are a few answers to common questions related to lightning.

*Why does lightning strike mountaintops and tall trees so often?* Simple, really. The farther things are away from the Earth, the closer they are to that step leader descending from the cloud, so they are more likely to be points at which the major discharge happens.

*Do lightning rods really work?* Sure. A lightning rod is nothing more than a metal rod placed on top of a house or building. This rod is connected with metal wire to the ground. It actually attracts the lightning bolt, but then provides an easy conducting path to safely divert the discharge away from the house or building. Once you know how a lightning rod works, you also know why it would be pretty stupid to stand out on a golf course with your metal golf club in the air during a thunderstorm. Without an easier path to take, which the wires connected to a lightning rod provide, the electric current goes right through your body. Not good.

*Where can you be safe from lightning?* Two of the safest places are in a car and in a plane. Both are made of metal, and electric currents tend to stay on the *outside* of metals, leaving you safe and sound inside your metal container. Of course, it would be a good thing *not* to be touching the outside of that car while you're riding along. I'd say the same for the airplane, but if you're touching the outside of a plane during a lightning storm, you have more problems than I can solve! ▪

# Why is a light-year a unit of distance rather than a unit of time?

There are lots of issues associated with measurement that can be confusing, so I'll use this opportunity to address several of them.

First, the light-year. It's easy to see why people think it must be a measurement of time because after all, the word *year* is in it. And of course, you will find that many people in everyday conversation use light-year as a measure of time, as in, "It will be light-years before everyone in the general populace learns how to properly pronounce the word *nuclear*." Okay, so what is a *light-year*? It's the distance that light travels in one year. Light travels pretty darned fast, so you might think that this is a big distance, and it is. Because light travels at a speed of $3 \times 10^8$ meters per second (that's three hundred million meters per second), or roughly seven times around the Earth

"A few more light-years?! That's what you said 15 minutes ago, Dad!"

in one second, this means that light travels about $9.5 \times 10^{15}$, or 9,600,000,000,000,000 meters, in a year. That's a lot of meters.

Scientists, and primarily astronomers, use the unit of light-years to measure distance simply because things are so far apart in the universe. Our nearest star, other than the Sun, is about four light-years away. So to avoid using numbers that are so large it's difficult to deal with them, we use light-years as a unit. And it's a distance, not a time.

## Scales and Such

Next up are a couple of measurement scales that can be misleading. We'll start with the Richter scale, which is used to measure the magnitude of earthquakes. If you have followed the news regarding earthquakes, you might know that an earthquake of magnitude 3 or 4 is minor, yet an earthquake of magnitude 7 or 8 means a big catastrophe. Seems silly, doesn't it? One earthquake poses no problem, but one twice as large is a major event. The key here is that the Richter scale is not linear but logarithmic.

I'll try to explain with a graph. Earthquakes can vary in size over a large range. One earthquake can be 10 times, 100 times, or even 10 million times stronger than another earthquake. So suppose you want to compare the strengths of various earthquakes over the past decade. The graph you create to display the strengths might look something

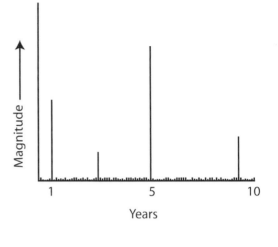

### Figure 1

## A linear scale representation of fictitious earthquake data

### Figure 2

## That same data presented in a logarithmic scale

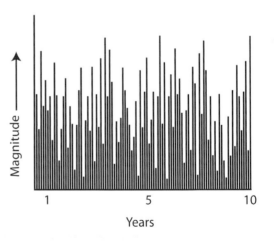

like Figure 1 (note that the data in Figures 1 and 2 are fictitious).

There's a problem with this graph. Because the range of magnitudes is so large, you can't view the small earthquakes on the same graph as the large earthquakes. If the large earthquakes are included in the graph, then the variations in the small ones are so tiny you can barely see them. Enter logarithms to help us. I'm not going to explain logarithms completely in this column, so I'll just provide a general picture. The logarithm of 10 is equal to 1, the logarithm of 100 is equal to 2, the logarithm of 1,000 is equal to 3, and so on. So if you have numbers that vary from 10 to 1,000, their logarithms vary only from 1 to 3. What this means is that huge differences in numbers can be reduced to a scale that is useful for comparison. When we change Figure 1 to a logarithmic graph, it looks like Figure 2.

And this is how a logarithmic scale such as the Richter scale can be misleading. An earthquake of 7 on the Richter scale seems to be not much larger than an earthquake of 6. Because the scale is logarithmic, though, the earthquake of magnitude 7 is 10 times stronger than an earthquake of magnitude 6. An earthquake of magnitude 8 is 100 times stronger than an earthquake of magnitude 6. An earthquake of magnitude 9 is 1,000 times stronger than an earthquake of magnitude 6. So two or three steps up on the scale might seem minor, but it's huge in reality.

## More Logarithmics

Another logarithmic scale is the pH scale, used for measuring the acidity of a solution. pH tells you the concentration of hydronium ions (basically the concentration of roaming protons). As with earthquakes, this concentration can vary over a large range. The range is so large that it's difficult to compare the concentrations. So we use the logarithmic

scale. A pH of 6 is 100 times more acidic than a pH of 8, and a pH of 4 is 10,000 times more acidic than a pH of 8. This is important for swimming pools, hot tubs, and aquariums. You might think that the fish in your aquarium are fine if the pH of the tank is only one, two, or three numbers above or below what it should be, but you're really dealing with 10 times the difference you're reading, or possibly 100 or 1,000 times the difference.

## Significant Figures

Finally, let's deal with all those numbers that appear on your calculator when you do a simple division or multiplication and how that relates to measurements. Suppose that for an experiment, you need to divide a large piece of metal into seven even pieces. The large piece of metal has a length of 14.37 meters, as measured by you. To figure out how long each piece should be, you divide the total length by the number of pieces and therefore do the following calculation on your calculator. You get this result:

$$14.37 / 7 = 2.05285714$$

So each piece should be 2.05285714 meters long. How are you going to measure each piece so precisely? The answer is that you don't have to, because most of those numbers in the final answer for the length of an individual piece are meaningless. Your measurement of the length of the original piece of metal was to the hundredths of a meter (the number was 14.37). There is no way that a calculation done from that measurement could be precise out to eight decimal places, as the number 2.05285714 implies. This is where mathematics and the real world part ways.

Topic: Units of Measurement
Go to: *www.scilinks.org*
Code: ASQ012

In math, numbers are numbers and are, in a sense, "pure." In the real world, we deal with measurements that have limitations. Depending on what tool we're using to measure something, the measurement can be precise to varying degrees. If you use a ruler to measure out a mile, that's not going to be as precise as using a tape measure, which will not be as precise as using surveying equipment. When you make calculations based on your measurements, the final result cannot be more precise than the least precise measurement you're using. In other words, the weakest link determines the quality of the final product. So if you are calculating the volume of a box, and you measure one of the sides of the box using your thumb to measure inches, the final volume will only be as precise as the measurement using your thumb, even if you used laser technology to measure the other sides.

For a thorough treatment of this idea, look up "significant figures" in your nearest math or science textbook. The bottom line is that your calculator relies on pure math, so don't always trust it for results in the real world. ■

# Why is Pluto no longer a planet?

On August 24, 2006, the International Astronomical Union (IAU) decided that Pluto is no longer a planet, but rather a *dwarf planet*. How did this happen? Did astronomers discover new information about Pluto? Did our understanding of the solar system undergo a radical change? Nah. It might seem that way, though. A few scientists seemed rather upset about the reclassification of Pluto, and many science educators have hailed this as a major change in scientific understanding.

Suddenly size mattered ...

You must be THIS big to ride The Solar System

IAU

Pluto

In recent years astronomers discovered a number of objects in the solar system that are similar to the dwarf planet formerly known as planet Pluto.

Topic: Pluto and Beyond
Go to: *www.scilinks.org*
Code: ASQ013

Topic: Classification
Go to: *www.scilinks.org*
Code: ASQ014

Our understanding of Pluto, however, did not change, nor did any great theories in astronomy undergo revision. What happened was that in recent years astronomers discovered a number of objects in the solar system that are similar to the dwarf planet formerly known as planet Pluto. There was a lot of debate about what to do—classify these other objects as planets or demote Pluto from planet status. The IAU chose the latter option. So all that changed was the set of criteria the IAU uses to classify objects as planets. No major theoretical change, but rather a somewhat arbitrary change in the rules. As such, the reclassification of Pluto doesn't reach the status of a significant change in the enterprise of science.

## Classification in Science

This brings up another question. What exactly is the role of classification in science? Is it always just an exercise in arbitrary rules? The short answer is no. Classification of things is an important part of doing science, even if it isn't a goal in and of itself. I'll use two examples to illustrate. First, we go back a few hundred years to when there were general, if not refined, theories of atoms. Many scientists were enamored with the notion that the universe is composed of elements and that each element is composed of a particular kind of atom. Scientists began to classify elements according to their properties and saw certain patterns. In the late 1800s, scientists

Meyer and Mendeleyev published different versions of the periodic table, which was a graphic representation of the patterns they saw among elements. In other words, they came up with a classification scheme. Mendeleyev was actually able to use this classification scheme to predict the existence of as-yet-undiscovered elements and was even able to predict their properties.

The periodic table was instrumental in helping scientists develop and refine our theory of atoms. We now have a relatively sophisticated theory of the atom that explains why various elements occupy particular positions in the periodic table. The main point is that our current understanding of atoms, including how electrons fill various energy levels, owes much to the original classification schemes that led to early versions of the periodic table.

## Whimsical Physicists

The second example is from high energy physics, so named because it involves the study of what happens when you use high energy particle accelerators to cause subatomic particles (particles smaller than atoms) to reach large speeds (near the speed of light) and then slam into other materials. When you do this, you get the creation of a whole bunch of new subatomic particles. In the early days of high energy physics (also known as particle physics because of all of the new particles), all physicists could do was classify the new particles according to their properties. There was, and still is, a major classification of particles into two groups, known as *bosons* and *leptons*. Within these groups, particles had proper-ties such as "charm" and "strangeness." Ah, those whimsical physicists! All of this classification and study of the properties of particles in each class eventually led to a theory of quarks that explained why particles fit into various categories. This is not unlike the development of the periodic table, followed by a theory that explained the classification scheme.

So classification as an end unto itself doesn't help further science a whole lot. Classification as a precursor to deeper understanding, though, is an important part of the development of scientific theories.

## Pluto's Significance

Okay, back to Pluto. Will the reclassification of Pluto lead to new theories? Doubtful, but the classification of objects in the universe in general has led to a greater understanding of all things astronomical, from how stars evolve to the age of the universe. The reclassification of Pluto could possibly play a small role in future understanding. In the meantime, the main effect of reclassifying Pluto has been cultural. Students are writing letters to the editor asking that their favorite planet be a planet again, and some people are actually upset that they now have to learn a new fact—that there are eight planets instead of nine. And of course, there are rumors that a particular cartoon mouse and his dog are justifiably ticked off. ▪

# Q Is it possible to turn coal into diamonds?

How cool would it be to be Lois Lane? Anytime she wants a diamond, she just has Superman use his super strength to squeeze a lump of coal. But is this really possible? Using a high enough temperature and enough pressure, can you turn coal into diamonds? To answer this, we have to address the nature and formation of coal and the nature and formation of diamonds. First, though, we have to talk about the carbon atom and what makes it so special.

## Carbon: One Unique Atom

There are more than 100 different kinds of atoms in the universe, and carbon stands out as a unique atom. It easily links up with other atoms because it has four electrons and four empty electron slots in its outer

"My carbon is too soft."

"My carbon is too impure."

"My carbon is just right."

shell (the outer shell of an atom refers to the outermost electrons that are available for sharing with other atoms). With these four electrons and four slots, carbon can hook up with other carbon atoms and with other kinds of atoms in many different ways. In other words, carbon is the basis for all sorts of different molecules. With the help of oxygen atoms, hydrogen atoms, and various other atoms, carbon is the main ingredient in substances that range from methane (the gas used in stoves and furnaces) to octane (a fuel) to polyester (for trendy leisure suits) to vinyl to … well, to lots and lots of substances, including many of the molecules that make up the human body.

Carbon can also link up solely with other carbon atoms. Again, because of the nature of carbon's outer electrons, carbon can form different kinds of structures. Graphite is one of the forms of pure car-

bon. Diamond is another, and there are two lesser-known forms of pure carbon. One is known as "white carbon," and the other form takes the name of "fullerenes" or "buckyballs," so named because this form is similar to the geodesic dome shape discovered by Buckminster Fuller. For the record, different structures that are composed of the same atom are called *allotropes*. So graphite, diamond, and the other two structures of carbon are allotropes of carbon. Also for the record, substances composed of "pure" carbon are never completely pure. Other atoms such as nitrogen sneak into these structures in varying degrees.

## Pencils Versus Diamonds

Let's focus on the prominent allotropes of carbon—graphite and diamond. Graphite is opaque (you can't see through it), is relatively soft, and flakes off easily. These properties make graphite a good thing to use in pencils (yep, it's graphite in your pencil "lead"). Diamond, on the other hand, is transparent and the hardest known

## Figure 1

The molecular structures of diamond (left) and graphite (right) determine their characteristic properties.

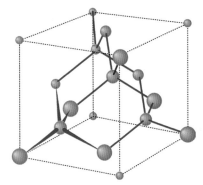
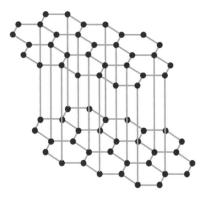

substance. The difference between graphite and diamond is solely due to the different way the carbon atoms connect together. Figure 1 shows the structures of both. Each small sphere in the drawings represents a carbon atom. In graphite, the carbon atoms group together in layers, leading to its "flaky" property. In diamond, the carbon atoms connect in a shape known as a "tetrahedron" that results in an overall cubic shape. The structure of diamond is especially sturdy. This leads to graphite and diamond having drastically different hardness, and it leads to light interacting with them in drastically different ways. Graphite rings never caught on because they just don't have that diamond sparkle.

Natural diamonds form deep underground, anywhere from 120 kilometers to 200 kilometers beneath the surface of the Earth. There the temperature and pressure are high enough to assemble carbon atoms into the particular structure of diamonds. Volcanic activity then brings diamonds near enough to the surface of the Earth that we can mine them. Most of the diamonds we mine are not pure enough for use in jewelry, so they're used in industry on diamond-tipped drills or saws (remember, diamonds are the hardest known substance). Of course, even gem-grade diamonds have impurities, and these impurities affect how light interacts with them. Completely pure diamond is clear, and diamonds with various impurities can be yellow, brown, or blue. The blue diamonds have many impurities, but they're also very expensive. Why? Because they're rare.

Okay, let's talk about creating diamonds artificially. Can you do it? Sure. At pressures and temperatures obtainable in the lab, we can take graphite and turn it into diamond. Makes sense, because graphite and diamond are both made of carbon atoms. Presently, artificial diamonds don't quite have the same qualities as natural diamonds, so don't start investing in pencil leads just yet. The process is improving, though, so it's possible that one day a jeweler won't be able to tell the difference between artificial and natural diamonds.

## So What About Coal?

I haven't said anything about coal yet, have I? That's because coal is not an allotrope of carbon. Coal forms over millions of years from the decayed remains of living things. As such, coal contains a lot of carbon, but it is by no means close to pure carbon. It has many atoms of oxygen, nitrogen, and other atoms. Coal contains anywhere from 50% to 90% carbon. So what happens if you use high temperatures and pressures to try and turn coal into diamond? You get lousy diamonds, with lots of impurities. Of course, coal is good for lots of other things, namely as a fuel for generating electricity and as an ingredient in the recipe for manufacturing many metals.

Where does this leave Lois Lane? Unfortunately, she turns out to be a cheap date because she accepts low-grade diamonds produced from coal that the guy in the cape gives her. As soon as he switches to squeezing pencils, though, Lois will be in business. ▩

# What causes the seasons?

Isn't it obvious? The Earth is close to the Sun in winter and far from the Sun in summer. No, wait … that's the wrong answer, even though it's a commonly held belief. Before we get to the correct answer, let's figure out why the first answer I gave is wrong. If being close to the Sun causes summer on Earth, then all parts of the Earth should experience summer at the same time. That doesn't happen, though. While it's summer in the Northern Hemisphere, it's winter in the Southern Hemisphere, and vice versa. Also, it turns out that the Earth is closest to the Sun in January and farthest from the Sun in July. If distance from the Sun determined the seasons in the Northern Hemisphere, shouldn't the Earth be closest to the Sun in July and farthest from the Sun in January? Yep. So throw that distance explanation out the window.

## Figure 1

## A Styrofoam ball model of Earth

Topic: What Causes Earth's Seasons?
Go to: *www.scilinks.org*
Code: ASQ016

## It's in the Tilt

To understand the correct answer, get a pencil or pen, a Styrofoam ball, and a flashlight. Skewer the Styrofoam ball with the pen or pencil and draw an "equator" on the ball so you have a tiny representation of the Earth. (See Figure 1.)

Turn on the flashlight and set it on a table so it shines on your model Earth.

Darken the room. Now tilt the "Earth" toward the flashlight and then away from the flashlight, noting how much light shines on the Northern Hemisphere in each case. (See Figure 2.)

If the flashlight were the Sun, you could say that when the Earth is tilted toward the Sun, the Northern Hemisphere receives a lot of direct sunlight, and when the Earth is tilted away from the Sun, the Southern Hemisphere receives a lot of direct sunlight and the Northern Hemisphere receives less sunlight. Now, if only the Earth were tilted, we would have

an explanation for the seasons. Lucky for us, the Earth is tilted at an angle of about 23.5 degrees with respect to its plane of orbit around the Sun. You can model this by replacing your flashlight with a table lamp with the shade removed, and then moving your Styrofoam Earth around the lamp as shown in Figure 3.

Note that the Earth always tilts in the same direction as it goes around the table-lamp Sun. At one point, the Northern Hemisphere is getting lots of direct sunlight, and on the opposite side of the orbit, the Southern Hemisphere is getting lots of

Figure 2

## How much light shines on different parts of the Earth for different tilts?

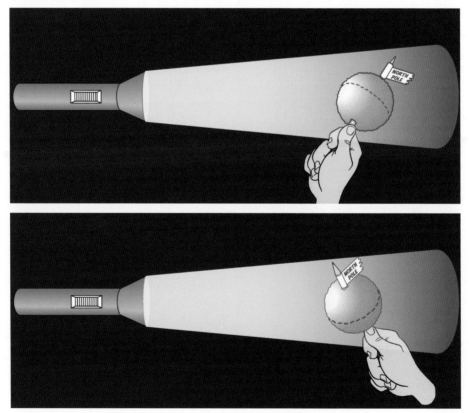

Figure 3

## Earth maintains a constant tilt as it moves around the Sun.

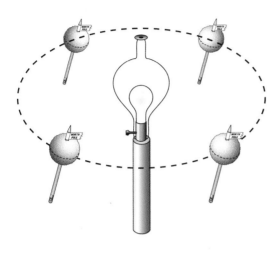

direct sunlight. Figure 4 shows a drawing (not to scale!) of the real Earth and Sun throughout the year.

### Shine On

Note that in fall and spring (Figure 4), sunlight hits all parts of the Earth the same—or does it? If that were true, wouldn't the North and South Poles be just as warm as the equator in fall and spring? Grab your flashlight again, and get a round balloon. Blow up the balloon and tie it off. Then shine the flashlight on the balloon from the side. First shine it on the center of the balloon and then move up and shine it

Figure 4

## The changing location of Earth in its revolution around the Sun results in the seasons.

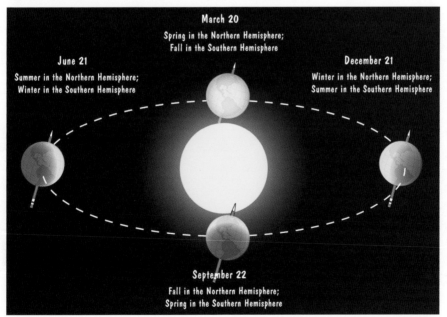

March 20
Spring in the Northern Hemisphere;
Fall in the Southern Hemisphere

June 21
Summer in the Northern Hemisphere;
Winter in the Southern Hemisphere

December 21
Winter in the Northern Hemisphere;
Summer in the Southern Hemisphere

September 22
Fall in the Northern Hemisphere;
Spring in the Southern Hemisphere

on the top part of the balloon, as in Figure 5.

Note that the light from the flashlight is more spread out when you shine it on the top part of the balloon and more concentrated when you shine it on the center of the balloon. This same thing happens with sunlight and the Earth. Sunlight hitting the equator is much more concentrated than sunlight hitting the poles, so the equator is always going to be warmer than the poles. See Figure 6.

So the tilt of the Earth is what causes the seasons, and uneven distribution of sunlight on the Earth keeps the poles cold and the equator warm. One last thing: The Earth does not always tilt in the same direction. The tilt of the Earth "precesses," or moves in a small circle, just as a spinning top does as it starts to slow down. What this means is that once the Earth is halfway through its precession, we'll have summer in January in the northern hemisphere! Not to worry, though. It takes about 26,000 years for the tilt of the Earth to complete one precession. Therefore, there won't be any significant calendar-season changes to make for at least the next 5,000 years. Time enough to adjust, I think. ■

### Resource
Robertson, W. 2005. *Air, water, and weather*. Arlington, VA: NSTA Press.

## Figure 5

### Light hitting a round object spreads out more in some places than in others.

## Figure 6

### Sunlight hitting the equator is always more concentrated than sunlight hitting the poles.

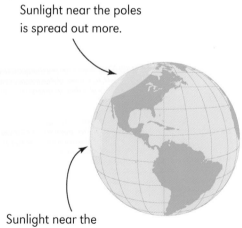

Sunlight near the poles is spread out more.

Sunlight near the equator is concentrated.

# How do we know the universe is expanding, and what exactly does that mean?

Unless you've been hiding out in a cave for the past 20 years, you've heard that the universe is expanding and it started with a big bang. To put an expanding universe in perspective, it helps to imagine that you live in a two-dimensional universe. There's a great book for helping you imagine this; it's called *Flatland* and was written in 1884 by Edwin A. Abbott. It's an amazing book of mathematical and scientific fiction and it's short, so by all means pick up a copy. Given that we can't

"I don't get it! That galaxy was right here last time!"

include a copy of the book here, I'll settle for explaining the major features of living in a two-dimensional (2–D) universe.

For your universe, let's use an infinitely large sheet of paper. Like the inhabitants of *Flatland*, you are a 2–D geometric shape such as a square or a triangle. Because the sheet of paper *is* your universe, you can only move around as long as you stay on the paper. In fact, for you the sheet of paper is all that exists. See Figure 1.

Imagine that you are approaching another person (another geometric shape) in your 2–D universe. No matter what the person's shape, he will appear to you as a straight line—you can only see the edges of the shape. If you read *Flatland*, you'll discover all the intricacies of living in this 2–D world, such as the fact that you can

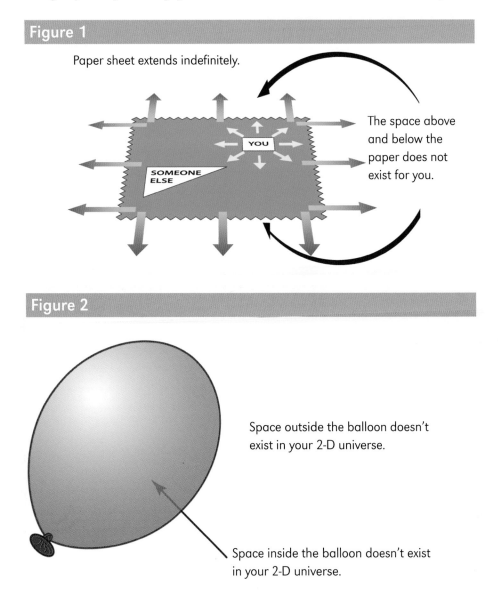

Figure 1

Paper sheet extends indefinitely.

YOU

SOMEONE ELSE

The space above and below the paper does not exist for you.

Figure 2

Space outside the balloon doesn't exist in your 2-D universe.

Space inside the balloon doesn't exist in your 2-D universe.

Figure 3

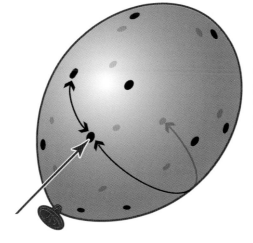

Measure the distances to other galaxies along the surface of the balloon.

Your galaxy

only tell someone's true shape by touching them to determine the angles of the shape or by using "shading" clues that are due to the fact that some parts of the person are farther from you than other parts. And for the sexist part of the book, you'll learn that females are lines rather than 2–D shapes. This leads to accidental stabbings when females approach others head on.

Okay, let's alter your 2–D universe a bit. Instead of a sheet of paper, imagine that you live on the surface of a balloon. It's still a 2–D universe, just a curved one. You and others living in this universe are unaware of the curvature, though. The inside and outside of the balloon *do not exist* for you. Check out Figure 2.

Of course, there are ways of knowing that you are living in a curved universe. For one thing, if you head off in one direction and travel long and far enough, you'll end up back where you started!

Time to model your 2–D universe with a real balloon. Blow up a round balloon a little bit and pinch off the opening, but don't tie it off. Using a marker, put

a bunch of more-or-less evenly spaced dots on the balloon. Choose one of the dots as your home galaxy and assume that the other dots represent other galaxies in the universe. See Figure 3. Measure the distance between your galaxy and other galaxies—some close to your galaxy and some far away from your galaxy (clearly there's a Star Wars joke in there somewhere). Because the inside and the outside of the balloon don't exist in your universe, you have to measure *along the surface of the balloon*. No fair taking a shortcut across the inside of the balloon.

Now expand your 2–D universe (blow up the balloon some more). As you do this, notice a couple of things. First, all of the galaxies (dots) move away from all the other galaxies. No matter what galaxy you're on, all the rest move away from you as the balloon universe expands. Second, the farther away another galaxy is from yours, the faster it moves away from you. To see this, measure the distances galaxies are from yours after you've blown up the

balloon. The ones farther from you will have moved a greater distance away from you than the ones closer to you. Look at Figures 4a and 4b.

To summarize, you have two clues that your curved 2–D universe is expanding. All objects in the universe are moving away from you, and the farther away the objects are, the faster they are moving away from you. The fact that your 2–D universe

## Figure 4a

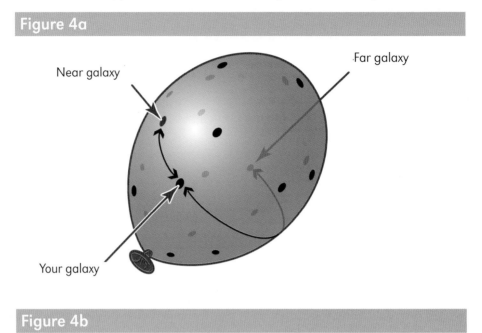

Near galaxy

Far galaxy

Your galaxy

## Figure 4b

As the universe expands, a far galaxy is moving away from you faster than a near galaxy.

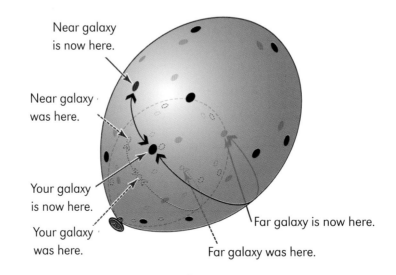

Near galaxy is now here.

Near galaxy was here.

Your galaxy is now here.

Your galaxy was here.

Far galaxy is now here.

Far galaxy was here.

is expanding is obvious to someone who lives in three dimensions, as we do. The balloon simply gets larger. It is expanding into three dimensions.

## Our Universe

I hope you know that we live not in a 2–D universe but in a 3–D universe. Astronomers have observed that all distant objects in our universe are moving away from us, and the farther away they are, the faster they're moving away from us. Sounds like an expanding universe, huh? The exact relationship between distance away and speed moving away is given by something called the *Hubble constant*, which you might have heard of.

How do astronomers know these things about the universe? Well, you need three bits of information—how far away things are, how fast they're moving, and in what direction they're moving. The simplest quantity—distance—is actually the most difficult to measure. It's complicated enough that I'm not even going to explain it here. Speed and direction, however, are relatively easy to measure. Think for a moment how a race car sounds as it passes you (you can hear this just watching a race on TV) or how a train sounds as it passes you. When these things are coming toward you, you hear a high pitch. When they're moving away, you hear a lower pitch. This change in pitch from high to low is noticeable just as the object passes by. This is known as the *Doppler effect,* and it's due to the source of sound "catching up" with the sound waves as the source approaches you and the source of sound "running away" from the sound waves as it recedes from you.

In addition to applying to sound waves, there's a Doppler effect for light waves.

When a light source moves toward you, the frequency of the light (corresponding to pitch in sound waves) is higher than if the light source isn't moving. When a light source moves away from you, the frequency of the light is lower than if the light source is stationary. Because blue light is a high frequency (for visible light) and red light is a low frequency, scientists refer to these motion-caused changes in frequency as *blue shifts* and *red shifts.* Suffice to say that the light we observe coming from distant objects in our universe is all red-shifted, indicating that all the distant objects are moving away from us. Also, the farther away the objects, the greater the red shift, which indicates a greater speed.

## So What Does It Mean?

We have a picture of what it's like for a 2–D universe to expand into three dimensions (3–D). Someone in three dimensions (us looking at the balloon universe) can easily see that this 2–D universe is expanding, but the people in that 2–D universe have to rely on other observations to determine that their universe is expanding. In our actual 3–D universe, we have made those same kinds of observations (distant objects moving away from us and the speed depending on distance), so we conclude that our 3–D universe is expanding. Anyone watching us from four dimensions could easily see that our universe is expanding, but we can't see it directly because our 3–D universe is expanding in four dimensions, just as the 2–D balloon universe was expanding in three dimensions.

Current theories have our universe being curved, just as the 2–D balloon is curved. Again, that curvature isn't obvious to us, just as the curvature of a very large balloon wouldn't be obvious to an ant

walking on it. We can conclude from that curvature, though, that our universe must have started from a very tiny universe (the universe is expanding, remember). We simply project back in time when our universe was basically a nothingness dot—that's the big bang.

Well, that's that. The best we can do to understand our expanding 3–D universe is to use an analogy with an expanding 2–D universe. The analogy is pretty good, though. For example, as on a 2–D balloon universe, you should be able to head off in one direction and eventually get back to where you started from, but from the opposite direction. Don't go trying to test that out, though. It would take billions of years even if you could travel at the speed of light. ■

## Reference

Abbott, E. A. 1992. *Flatland: A romance of many dimensions.* Unabr. ed. Minneola, NY: Dover.

# Q: Why are oceans salty and lakes and rivers not?

For starters, lakes and rivers do contain salt, just not as much as the oceans. If you take a glass of drinking water and add a few grains of table salt, chances are you won't taste that salt in the water. So-called freshwater in lakes and oceans also contains many other dissolved minerals. Just for kicks, get some distilled water and have a drink. You will undoubtedly notice a difference in taste between that and your regular drinking water. That's because distilled water has many of the natural salts and minerals removed. In some areas, drinking water contains relatively large quantities of dissolved minerals, which can result in

"Sorry, we're out of grog, honey. But we have plenty of water—distilled, fresh, and ocean."

rust-colored stains in your sink and mineral buildup in pipes. And, if you need further convincing of the mineral content of freshwater, I can direct you to a cabin in northern Michigan where I once spent the summer. The water out of the tap was rust colored and smelled of sulfur—great for baths! Anyway, the question is not why oceans are salty and lakes and rivers are not, but rather *why* the oceans are so much saltier than lakes and rivers.

## Inlets and Outlets

To understand what's going on, try this simple activity. Dissolve a handful of table salt in a pan of water, and then either leave the pan out until the water evaporates or heat the pan up so the water boils away. What you'll be left with is a bunch of salt in the pan. This illustrates that when water evaporates, any dissolved salt or minerals are left behind (not completely true, or else you wouldn't be able to "smell the salt air" near an ocean). That's fine, but since water evaporates from lakes and rivers as well as from oceans, this must not tell the whole story.

Now find a map of your state or region that shows lakes and rivers. Notice that virtually all of the small streams empty into larger rivers, which either empty into rivers that lead to the ocean or empty into lakes. Notice also that lakes have rivers entering them, and rivers leaving them— an inlet and an outlet. Now, what

## Figure 1

# A path to the ocean

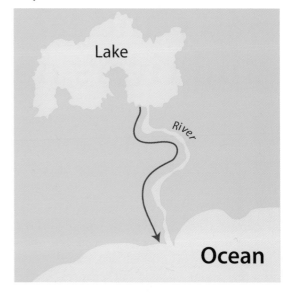

## Figure 2

# A "landlocked" lake

is the main source of water for streams and rivers? Rainfall and runoff that is a result of rainfall. This rainfall does contain salts and minerals but not much. The runoff from snow melting and rain falling in mountains contains a bit more in the way of salts and minerals because it interacts with rocks on the way down, so it would be wrong to say that rivers and lakes don't have salts and minerals entering them. But there's not much buildup. Why? Because a large portion of those salts and minerals washes downstream into other rivers, or through the outlet stream or river of a lake, and eventually winds up in the oceans. So the answer to why rivers and lakes are not as salty as the oceans is that salts and minerals that enter have an avenue for escape, which is a path to the oceans (Figure 1).

Oceans don't have an outlet, though. The primary way that water leaves the oceans is through evaporation, and that process leaves salts and minerals behind. No outlet means a buildup of those things, and a salty ocean. A confirmation of this mechanism is found in the Great Salt Lake in Utah (Figure 2). The Great Salt Lake is ... um ... salty. Why? No outlet stream or river. Water leaves the Great Salt Lake through evaporation, and just as with the

oceans, that process leaves a salt and mineral buildup behind.

## Why So Salty?

If you figure out the contribution of rivers to the saltiness of the oceans over the history of the Earth (and people have done this!), you can't account for all of the dissolved salts and minerals in the oceans. Turns out there are other sources, some of which are not all that well understood. One indication that the sources of salt in the ocean are not simple is the composition of sea salt. It's not just sodium and chlorine, as you find in table salt, but also includes calcium, potassium, magnesium, and many, many more chemicals. In the formation of the Earth's crust, escaping gases and magma infused oceans with a great many salts and minerals. Even today, volcanic eruptions that spill into the oceans contribute to the ocean's salinity. The wide variety of marine life also appears to contribute to the salt and mineral content of the oceans, through the decay of the organisms themselves and the shells many of them leave behind. So it appears that the oceans began as slightly salty, and the "fresh" water from rivers just continues to make them saltier.

Now, I don't know about you, but I'm hungry for a potato chip. ■

# Physical Science

# Q: How do we know protons, electrons, and quarks really exist?

Scientific explanations often make use of things we cannot see or feel, such as protons, electrons, and quarks. Do these things really exist? If so, how do we know they exist?

Imagine you're enclosed in a completely dark room with no light at all and can't see a thing. You are chained to a chair somewhere in the room, and you have a pile of rocks at your disposal. While trying to decide whether or not you are part of a bad horror film, you decide to figure out the size of the room you're in and its shape.

Good thing you have those rocks. You can throw the rocks in all directions. Judging from how long it takes for a rock to hit a wall in a particular direction, you can get a rough idea of how far away the walls are.

It's *not* here if I don't see it!
It's *not* here if I don't see it!
It's *not* here if I don't see it!
Right, Bob? ... Bob?

Topic: Atoms
Go to: www.scilinks.org
Code: ASQ017

If you have enough rocks and patience, you can probably get a good idea of what sort of room you're in. If there's a door (no doubt handy if you actually *are* in a horror film), you can probably tell where the door is by the different sound made when the rocks hit it.

## That's "Consistent With" ...

Suppose it is not possible to ever turn on the lights in the room. Can you be 100% certain the walls are where you think they are? Was that really a door that you hit? For that matter, can you be completely certain those were walls you hit? Is it possible that the sounds were made by something else?

No, you can't be 100% certain your surroundings are what you think they are, because you can never turn on the lights to see for sure. One thing you *can* say, though, is that all of your observations (i.e., the sounds you heard) are *consistent with* there being walls at varying distances away from you. You could even draw a map of your room. You could use the time of travel for the rocks thrown in each direction to estimate how far away the walls are in each direction. Abrupt changes in wall distance might be difficult to determine, so your map might be a bit fuzzy near those changes, but you still could get a general idea.

Let's move on to atoms—those tiny little things that you've heard about since you were in the second grade. You've seen drawings of atoms. How did people decide what those drawings should look like? Part of the answer has to do with experiments similar to throwing rocks at the walls of a dark room.

In a famous experiment performed in the early twentieth century, Ernest Rutherford fired alpha particles (other tiny things you can't see!) at gold foil and looked at the pattern the particles made after hitting the foil. This pattern indicated that the atoms of gold had a closely packed, positively charged nucleus. The reasoning behind this picture of an atom had to do with the fact that alpha particles are positively charged and would be repelled by a positively charged nucleus. Although most alpha particles went straight through the gold foil, some "bounced off" at sharp angles, even to the point of heading back in the direction from which they came. Only a closely packed, positively charged nucleus of a gold atom could accomplish this.

This experiment, plus many others like it, plus observations of chemical reactions, nuclear reactions, and the light that substances emit, all combine to give us a particular picture of what atoms look like. Just as with that dark room in which you can't turn on the lights, though, we cannot isolate a single atom and look directly at it to see if our drawings are correct.

The important thing is that everything we observe is *consistent with* our current view of atoms. The same statement goes for all sorts of other scientific models, such as quarks, electric and magnetic fields, and black holes. They're useful models because they explain our observations and help us predict new observations.

## Who Needs Reality?

What about the issue of whether or not these models are real? Are electrons real? Are atoms even real? Fortunately for us, it doesn't matter whether or not these things are real. If you ask this question of a room full of scientists, you will find some who say these models are so well supported by evidence that they are, in fact, real. You will also find some who say these models are just constructs that have been invented by people. All of those scientists, however, make use of the models. Your philosophy regarding the reality of models doesn't affect your ability to use the models to guide your scientific investigations. If you believe these models represent reality, great. If you don't believe these models represent reality, also great. You can use the models effectively no matter what you believe.

Finally, how does this issue apply to your classroom teaching? Well, for starters it makes for a great classroom discussion. It does more than that, though. It helps put the knowledge of science into perspective. A great physics educator by the name of Arnold Arons has argued that two of the most important questions we can ask in the teaching of science are, "How do we know?" and "Why do we believe?" If you weave those questions into your science lessons, you will help students see science as much more than a collection of facts and formulas.

Now *there's* something worth doing! ∎

# Q: Why does a color change indicate a chemical change?

A: There are a number of indicators you can use to determine whether or not a chemical reaction has occurred. Among them are a change in color, the evolution of a gas, and the production or absorption of heat. To understand why any of these indica- tors works, we first need to under- stand what we mean by a *chemical reaction*, so let's start there. In fact, let's begin with something more basic, which is our scientific model for what makes different substances have different properties.

"It's still a white sweater.... It's just radiating more pink than the other colors."

## Old Substance, New Substance

Water, paper, air, and glass all have distinct properties. These distinct properties are due to the fact that these substances are composed of different atoms and molecules and often have different arrangements of those atoms and molecules. Water is composed of a particular combination of hydrogen and oxygen atoms, and air is composed primarily of nitrogen molecules and oxygen molecules. As an example of different arrangements of atoms leading to different substances, consider graphite and diamond. Both are composed solely of carbon atoms, but their different arrangements of those atoms lead to quite different properties (and price!).

When we begin with one or more substances and end up with different substances, we say that a *chemical reaction* has occurred. When you combine the element sodium with chlorine gas under the right conditions, for example, you end up with sodium chloride (table salt). Intense heat and pressure can cause graphite to form into diamond (just ask Superman how to do this). Both of these are examples of chemical reactions because a new substance forms. (See "Is it possible to turn coal into diamonds?" p. 89.)

## Light Matters

To understand how color change indicates that a chemical reaction occurred, you first need to know about how light interacts with matter. First of all, white light, which is what we usually use to see things, is composed of all colors. When this white light comes in contact with an object, the atoms and molecules in that object absorb the light and then radiate, or give off, some or all of it. Different atoms and molecules radiate different colors of light, and the colors they radiate depend on their particular atomic and molecular structure. To be more precise, it's the electrons in those atoms that interact with the light. A white shirt radiates all of the light that hits it. A yellow shirt radiates primarily yellow light, and a black shirt absorbs most of the light that hits it. The reason these shirts radiate different colors is that the dyes in the shirts have different molecular structures.

## Sometimes Color Changes...

Now consider a chemical reaction in which two or more substances combine, resulting in one or more new substances. The new substances have different molecular structures from the original substances. Because of this different molecular structure, it is quite possible that the new substances absorb and then radiate light differently from how the original substances absorbed and then radiated light. Thus, there might be a color change.

One such color change you might have seen as a high school student is when you add a base such as sodium hydroxide to the chemical phenolphthalein. The phenolphthalein is clear before you add the base, and it turns pink after you add it. The molecular structure of the phenolphthalein changes slightly in this process, resulting in the new color.

## ... Sometimes Not

Of course, it's possible that there won't be a color change at all. Even though you are creating new molecular structures in a chemical reaction, that doesn't mean the new structures will radiate light any differently from how the original structures radiated light. For example, adding vinegar

Topic: Physical/Chemical Changes
Go to: *www.scilinks.org*
Code: ASQ018

to baking soda creates a familiar foaming action but does not involve a color change. Of course, the foaming action indicates the release of a gas (carbon dioxide), so we do know a chemical reaction has taken place.

So does a color change always mean you have observed a chemical reaction? Nope. Put red food coloring in a glass of water and put blue food coloring in another glass of water. Then pour the two glasses of colored water together (might want to get a bigger glass for this!). Is there a color change? Sure. You now have purple water. There was no chemical reaction, however. All that happened was the red and blue water samples *dissolved* in each other. When a substance dissolves in water, the substance retains its molecular identity and simply mixes throughout the water. As such, our new glass of water contains water, red food coloring, and blue food coloring. You haven't created any new molecules. That new color you see is a result of the combined absorption and radiation of white light by the separate molecules in the red and blue food coloring. If a chemical reaction had taken place, then the structure of the molecules in the food coloring and/or the water would have been altered.

Students in elementary and middle school who study chemical reactions often don't learn much beyond the indicators that a chemical reaction has occurred. While these indicators are useful, they don't go very far in explaining what has happened in the chemical reactions. If your students have at least some idea of why these indicators work, they'll gain a deeper understanding of the process. ■

# Q: Why does air expand when you heat it, and why does hot air rise?

A: The short answers to these questions are that air doesn't necessarily expand when you heat it, and hot air doesn't always rise. These are two commonly misunderstood concepts related to the behavior of gases and how this behavior applies to physical situations, including weather.

## Expanding Air?

I'll begin with an incorrect explanation for why air (or any other gas, for that matter) expands when you heat it. The reason I'm doing this is that the following *wrong* explanation can be found in many science resources.

> *Hot air molecules, on average, have more space between them than cool air molecules. Therefore, when you heat air it expands to allow more space for the molecules. If you then cool the air, it contracts because cool air molecules need less space than hot air molecules.*

To see why this is an incorrect explanation, imagine a bunch of gas molecules bouncing around inside a rigid container. They move at a constant speed until they run into another molecule or the walls of the container. In collisions, the molecules bounce off one another and off the walls like billiard balls. The molecules in a cool gas move slower, on average, than do molecules in a hot gas. This model is

"If he's full of hot air, how come he doesn't float away?"

part of what is known as the kinetic theory of gases, and as a first approximation, it does a good job of explaining what gases do. Figure 1 shows a few gas molecules doing this.

Now let's take a top view of this process. We have molecules bouncing around and using up the available space within the rigid walls (see Figure 2).

Let's assume these molecules are part of a cool gas. They're moving fast because that's what gas molecules do, but they're moving slower than the molecules in a hot gas. How much of the space inside our container are the molecules using? All of it. No part of this container is somehow off limits, so it's safe to say that the gas takes up all of the available space. Now let's heat the gas. That makes the molecules move faster. As a result, they hit the container harder and more often. Does the gas expand, though? Nope. The walls are rigid, so the gas uses the same space whether the gas is hot or cool. Now look back at Figure 1. Can you tell whether the gas is hot or cool from that snapshot of what's going on? No.

The bottom line here is that the molecules in a hot gas do not require any more room than a cool gas, and a cool gas does not require less room than a hot gas. So heating a gas does not necessarily cause the gas to expand, and cooling it does not cause the gas to contract. But heating a gas does usually cause it to expand, right? Right. That's because for many situations, including virtually all applications in weather, the container for the gas is not rigid. If our gas were in a balloon, heating it would cause the molecules inside to move faster and hit the balloon harder and more often, and the balloon would expand. If we then cool the gas, the molecules don't hit the balloon as hard and hit it less often, so the balloon contracts and causes the gas to contract.

So, yes, heating a gas most often causes it to expand and cooling a gas most often causes it to contract, but this has almost everything to do with whatever is surrounding the gas (a rigid or flexible container) rather than the gas itself. There is no inherent need for the molecules in a hot gas to have more space and no inherent need for cool gas molecules to have less space.

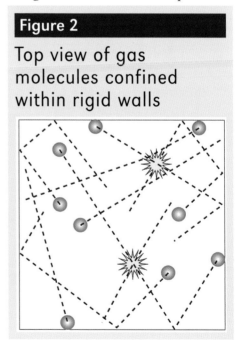

### Figure 2

Top view of gas molecules confined within rigid walls

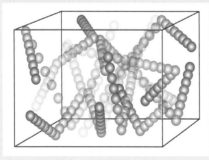

### Figure 1

How gas molecules behave

# Hot Air Rising?

Time for another incorrect explanation. When dealing with weather, it is common to discuss what are known as *convection cells,* in which hot air is rising and cold air is sinking, as in Figure 3.

Here's the *incorrect* explanation, which again you can find in many science resources.

## Figure 3

### A convection cell

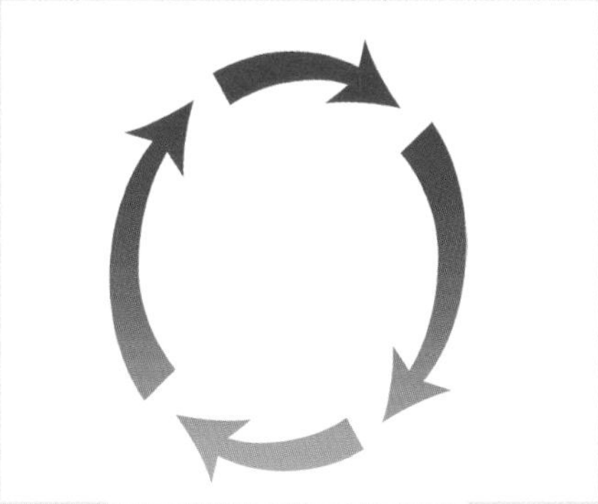

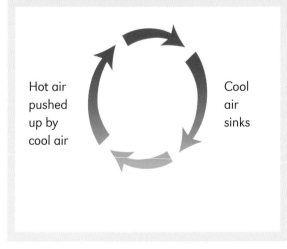

## Figure 4

### The mechanism behind a convection cell

Hot air pushed up by cool air

Cool air sinks

*A pocket of hot air is surrounded by cooler air. As the hot air rises, the cool air rushes in to take its place. As that cool air that rushed in heats up, it rises, and again outside cooler air rushes in to take its place. This is the basic mechanism of a convection cell.*

Imagine you have a pocket of hot air somewhere on Earth, with no other air around it. Why in the world would that hot air rise? The hot air molecules have mass and are attracted to Earth by the force of gravity. Those molecules are moving about randomly, so naturally they will move out in all directions (no rigid container!), but there is no reason to expect them to spontaneously move upward.

Back to the hot air surrounded by cooler air. Because the air surrounding the hot air can "give," the faster moving molecules in the hot air will push on their surroundings and create more space for themselves. This makes the hot air less dense than the surrounding, cooler air. When you submerge a less-dense substance in a more dense substance, the more dense substance exerts an upward force on the less dense substance.

Think about blowing up a balloon and submerging it in your bathtub. The water is denser than the balloon plus its air inside, so the water pushes the balloon upward. Exactly why the more dense water pushes up on the balloon, and why surrounding cool air pushes up on hot air, takes a bit more space than we have here. It has to do with the force of gravity and how the weight of air or water above a certain point exerts a force on objects at that point. The name for the force exerted is the *buoyant* force. At any rate, the proper diagram to explain a convection cell is shown in Figure 4 (p. 119). The denser cool air exerts an upward buoyant force on the less dense hot air. This is what makes the hot air rise. So hot air rising and cold air rushing in to take its place is wrong; the sinking cold air is what pushes the hot air up.

## What's the Point?

Maybe you're asking why it makes a difference whether the explanation of an event is correct or not. After all, the result is the same. Heated air does expand (usually) and hot air does rise (no matter what the cause). Well, it doesn't make a difference—unless you want scientific concepts to make sense. I have encountered many people who, when I bring up the subject, want to know why in the world heated air should expand and why in the world hot air should rise. It's all about making science make sense, which is what we should all demand of scientific explanations. ■

# Q: What exactly is energy?

A: Seems like a simple question, so you might expect a simple answer. For that simple answer, let's head to your average science textbook and retrieve the following: "Energy is the ability to do work."

Okay, but what does that mean? What do we mean by *work*? Even if we know what work is, does that give us a good feel for what *energy* is? Is energy something tangible, like a rock? Can you hold an energy

STUNT MAN STAN

SLINGSHOT ACROSS THE CANYON

"Stan, I may have miscalculated the potential energy.... Stan?"

in your hand? Is energy something we can model in the same way we draw models of atoms or representations of magnetic field lines?

## It's Kinetic or Potential

Before we answer those questions, let's back up a bit and discuss a few basics. First, it's relatively easy to recognize when something has energy. Anything that's moving has energy, and the faster the object is moving, the more energy it has. Also, the more massive a moving object, the more energy it has. A semi-truck moving at 60 miles per hour has more energy than a Yugo moving at 60 miles per hour. For the record, we call the energy an object has because of its motion *kinetic energy* (so named because the Greek word *kinesis* means motion).

Things that aren't moving also have energy. A charged-up battery has energy. A boulder poised at the edge of a cliff has energy. A stretched rubber band or spring has energy. Two magnets that have been pulled apart have energy (watch them snap back together when you let go). In these latter examples, the objects have energy because of their relative shape and/or position. The battery has energy because of the arrangement of dissimilar substances such as carbon and zinc; the rubber band and spring have energy because of their shape; and the magnets and the boulder (include the Earth here because gravity is important) have energy because of their position. Energy that is a result of relative shape and/or position is called *potential energy*.

## A Conserved Quantity

It turns out that all kinds of energy—sound energy, light energy, chemical energy, nuclear energy, and on and on—fit into the two categories of kinetic energy and potential energy. That simplifies things a bit, but you might be aware that even with these two categories, there are lots of formulas one can use to calculate energy. Why calculate amounts of energy? Because by using formulas to keep track of energy as it moves from one place to another, we can better understand how various living and nonliving things interact with one another. If we understand the energy transformations throughout an ecosystem, then we know more about the organisms living there. If we understand how potential energy transforms to kinetic energy and back, then we know how to design a roller coaster.

Okay, great. We have this abstract thing called energy, and we have formulas for calculating the energy of objects as energy takes on different forms. One more thing will help us understand what energy is, and that thing is the fact that energy (as represented by all these formulas) is a *conserved quantity*. Before explaining what that means, I need to explain to you what a *closed system* is. A closed system is a collection of objects surrounded by an imaginary boundary. If the system is closed, then no energy crosses the boundary in either direction, in or out. Imagine a perfect thermos that doesn't let heat in or out. This would be a closed system. A perfectly oiled machine that loses absolutely no energy due to friction would also be a closed system. Of course, it's practically impossible to create a truly closed system, but the concept is useful. If we were able to create a closed system, with no energy in or out, the total energy possessed by all the objects in the system would be *constant*—always the

Topic: Kinetic and Potential Energy
Go to: www.scilinks.org
Code: ASQ019

Topic: Law of Conservation of Energy
Go to: www.scilinks.org
Code: ASQ020

same total number. Objects transfer energy to other objects, and the energy changes form continuously (from one kind of kinetic energy to another, from kinetic energy of one object to potential energy of other objects, etc.). During these transformations, the total energy is constant, and that is a very useful thing for figuring what objects are doing now and what they will be doing in the future. And in case you didn't know, figuring out what objects are doing and what they will do in the future is what much of science is about. This applies to satellites in orbit, electrons hanging around atoms, the operation of ecosystems, the operation of animal body systems, and roller coasters negotiating a loop successfully.

So what is energy? It's this abstract, conserved quantity that helps us solve a multitude of science problems. No, you can't hold an energy in your hand, and you can't draw a picture of an energy, but you can use the idealized concept of a closed system, plus the fact that energy is conserved in a closed system, to analyze many situations.

## The Work-Energy Theorem

To finish, I really should explain how one calculates formulas for different types of energy. There is something called the work-energy theorem, which states that the total work done on an object is numerically equal to the change in kinetic energy of the object. We write that as follows:

Total work done = change in kinetic energy

We use a special definition of work for this theorem. Work is defined as the net (total) force applied to an object multiplied by the distance the object moves in the direction of the force. I don't expect to be able to explain fully the concept of work in this brief column, so we'll focus on the results of the work-energy theorem. If you apply a single force to an object for a short length of time, calculating the work done on the object (using a little bit of calculus) results in the expression $\frac{1}{2}mv^2$, which is a formula for kinetic energy that you might recognize. By carefully considering the work done by certain kinds of forces, we can also end up with formulas that represent different kinds of potential energy. The most important result, though, is that the work-energy theorem leads directly to the realization that energy is a conserved quantity. In this sense, the work-energy theorem is what really tells us what energy is.

We can also analyze the work-energy theorem in reverse. If you do work on something to give it energy, it sort of makes sense that an object that has energy can do work for you. Just imagine a bowling ball that has lots of kinetic energy. It has the ability to do work (exert a force on something in the direction of the thing's motion) on the bowling pins. So we have the expression "energy is the ability to do work." Now, doesn't that ease your mind? ■

# Q: How can an ocean liner made of steel float on water?

A: Sinking and floating is a subject covered in many science classes, from kindergarten through college physics. Even the audiences of late-night talk shows get to predict whether an object will sink or float in water. And of course, we all know that witches will float if they weigh the same as a duck (Monty Python reference). Yet one of the most common examples of sinking and floating seems to go against common sense.

"On the bright side, we know the gravitational force was much greater than the buoyant force!"

How can something made of steel—a heavy metal—float in water? Let's figure it out.

## A Fluid's Force

Water, and any other fluid for that matter, exerts an upward force on anything submerged in it. To see that, construct a crude balance using slotted craft sticks, paper clips, and washers, as shown in Figure 1. Be sure to hold two craft sticks side by side to support the top craft stick, or you'll have a difficult time keeping things in balance.

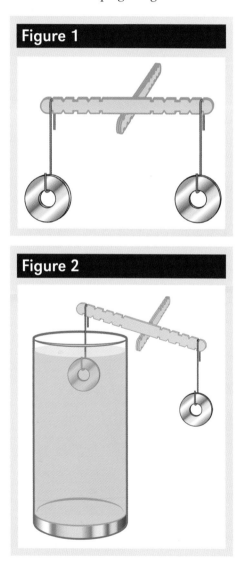

**Figure 1**

**Figure 2**

Now dip one of the washers in a glass of water. That washer moves up, correct (Figure 2)?

You can interpret this result in two ways. One is to conclude that objects simply weigh less when immersed in water. The other is to conclude that water pushes up on objects immersed in it. Given that no one has yet figured out how to manipulate the force of gravity, we're going to accept the second conclusion. There's a name for the force a fluid exerts on objects immersed in it. That name is the *buoyant force*. So normally, an object partially or fully immersed in a fluid experiences two main forces—gravity pulling down (toward the center of the Earth) and the buoyant force pushing up (in the direction opposite to the direction of gravity).

The relative size of these two forces determines whether an object will sink, float, or shoot upward in water. If the gravitational force is larger than the buoyant force, the object sinks. If the gravitational force and the buoyant force are equal, the object floats. If the buoyant force is larger than the gravitational force, the object shoots upward (Figure 3).

## More Than Density

Simple enough so far, right? Yes, but here's where people are likely to mess up when dealing with sinking and floating. Common sense tells us that all we really have to worry about is the density of the object and the density of water. By density, I mean how closely packed the object is. In more rigorous terms, the density of an object is its mass divided by its volume. Lots of mass in a small volume leads to a large density, and little mass in a large volume leads to a small density. If the object is denser than water, it makes sense that the

National Science Teachers Association

object should sink when placed in water. For example, a penny is denser than water and, sure enough, a penny sinks in water. If the object is less dense than water, it should either float on the surface of the water or even shoot upward when completely immersed in water. This does, in fact, happen with objects such as Styrofoam balls and corks. Before going on, we know that this analysis doesn't always "hold water," so to speak. That ocean liner we're talking about is made of steel, which is a very dense substance. Yet, it floats in water.

The above analysis does work when dealing only with liquids. Oil is less dense than water, and oil floats on water. Alcohol is also less dense than water, so alcohol also floats on water. Chocolate syrup is denser than milk, so the chocolate syrup I pour in my milk sinks to the bottom (the milk floats on the syrup). So less dense liq-uids always float on denser liquids. Not so simple with objects in liquids, though, because the buoyant force on an object depends on things other than the density of the object.

Topic: Buoyancy
Go to: www.scilinks.org
Code: ASQ021

For our first clue into how the buoyant force works, get two identical balloons. Blow one balloon up a little bit, and blow the other one up a lot. Tie both of them off. By holding these balloons in your hands, try to convince yourself that they weigh about the same. If you were to use a delicate pan balance, you could do a better job of convincing yourself they weigh the same even though they're different sizes. Now submerge both balloons in a sink or tub of water and let them go. Which one shoots up the highest? Which one do you sup-

## Figure 3

## Buoyant force

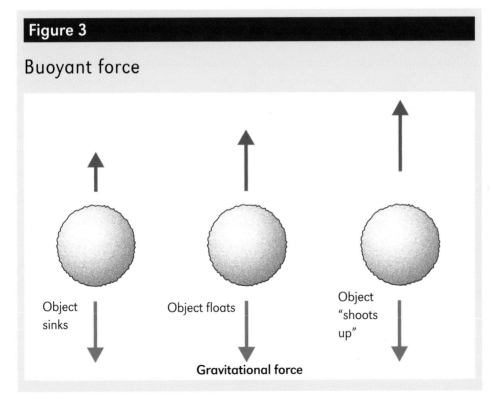

Object sinks

Object floats

Object "shoots up"

**Gravitational force**

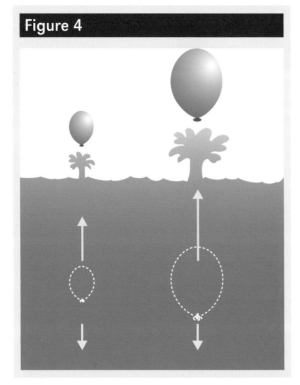

Figure 4

Place the ball first in the water and then in the vege-table oil. As you do this, notice how "high up" the ball floats in each liquid. The ball should float lower (is submerged a bit more) in the vegetable oil than it does in the water. Remember that vegetable oil is less dense than water. This illustrates the second piece of the buoyant force puzzle, which is:

The buoyant force a fluid exerts on an object depends on the density of the fluid. The denser the fluid, the larger the buoyant force.

If you've ever been to the Great Salt Lake and gone for a swim, you've experienced this principle. Saltwater is denser than freshwater, so saltwater exerts a larger buoyant force on you than freshwater does. Thus, it is much easier to float in the Great Salt Lake than it is in a freshwater lake. You naturally float "higher up" in saltwater. For something that doesn't require traveling to Utah, simply put an egg in a cup of water. The egg sinks. Gradually add salt to the water and stir so the salt dissolves. Once you have added enough salt (it takes quite a bit), the egg will float. What has happened is that you have increased the density of the fluid, thus increasing the size of the buoyant force to the point that it is equal to the gravitational force pulling down on the egg.

One science activity that is popular in elementary school is using clay to make boats. Place a ball of clay in a tub of water and it sinks. Shape the ball of clay into a rudimentary boat, and you can get it to float. In changing the shape of the clay, you haven't appreciably changed the density of the clay. The boat is basically the

pose experienced a greater upward buoyant force from the water? If you said the larger balloon experienced a larger buoyant force, give yourself a gold star. Figure 4 shows the balloons and the size of the forces acting on each. Note that the gravitational forces are the same (the balloons weigh the same) and that the buoyant force on the large balloon is greater than the buoyant force on the small balloon.

This little activity illustrates an important piece of the buoyant force puzzle, which is:

The buoyant force a fluid exerts on an object depends on how much of the fluid the object displaces. The more fluid the object displaces, the larger the buoyant force.

Now get yourself a Styrofoam ball or some other object that floats easily, a glass of water, and a glass of vegetable oil.

same density as the ball of clay. However, you have changed the clay so the boat displaces more water than the ball of clay. This increased displacement increases the buoyant force that the water exerts on the clay (Figure 5).

## The Shape of Things

What works for clay boats works for ocean liners. If you take a large hunk of steel and throw it into the ocean, it will head down and say hi to Davy Jones. If you shape this steel into a boat that displaces a lot of water, though, the buoyant force from the water will be large enough to equal the gravitational force on the steel, and you have a floating object. Of course, I also explained that the density of the fluid is important. If you have a clay boat that barely floats in water, expect this same boat to sink in a tub of less dense fluids such as vegetable oil or alcohol. If you have an ocean liner that barely floats in the ocean, expect this same ocean liner to sink if you travel to less-dense freshwater. And this is the primary reason why ocean liners don't travel up the Mississippi River. Well, actually, this might be the primary reason if ocean liners could fit in the Mississippi River! ■

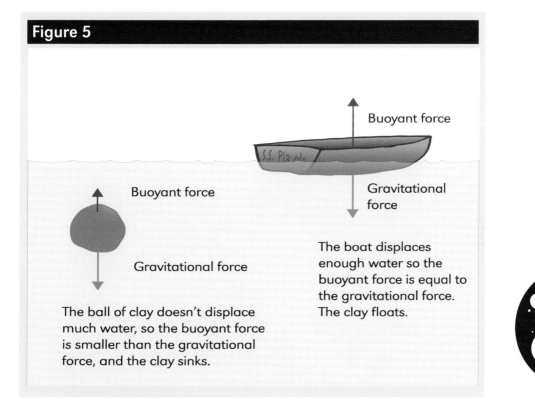

### Figure 5

Buoyant force

Buoyant force

Gravitational force

The boat displaces enough water so the buoyant force is equal to the gravitational force. The clay floats.

Gravitational force

The ball of clay doesn't displace much water, so the buoyant force is smaller than the gravitational force, and the clay sinks.

# Why are there so many different models of light?

Is light a ray, a wave, or a particle? Yes, yes, and yes. There are three viable models for light, each appropriate for different situations. I'll discuss the situations to which each applies, and then discuss how these different explanations are all compatible with one another.

## The Ray Model

Light is often represented as a bunch of rays, as illustrated in Figure 1 (p. 132). In

"Yes, Birdboy, you might think it's a ray traveling in a straight line. Actually, though, the laser light spreads out slightly as it ..."

fact, this is pretty much the only model used for light in elementary and middle school textbooks.

In this model, light travels in straight lines until it hits something, at which point it's reflected or absorbed. We can use this model to explain shadows; the relationship between incident and reflected angles; how a pinhole camera works; and how systems of lenses such as those found in telescopes, microscopes, and binoculars work. Figure 2 shows a few "ray diagrams" associated with these applications.

If the ray model of light explained *all* the behaviors of light, there wouldn't be a need for any other models. To see for yourself how the ray model doesn't explain everything, try the following activities. First, shine a flashlight on a wall and then place an object with a smooth edge (a ruler or index card will work) in the path of the light. Check out the shadow cast by this object. Is it a sharp, clean shadow? Most likely not. For your next activity, get two index cards and head to the store to find a lightbulb with a long, thin filament like the one shown in Figure 3a (p. 134).

Put your fashionable new lightbulb in a table lamp and remove the lamp shade. Then look at the bulb through the slit formed by the two cards as you bring them together. Narrow that slit until you see an interesting pattern of light and dark lines spread out from the slit. See Figures 3a and 3b (p. 134).

The ray model of light doesn't explain what you observed if you did the activities I told you to do. If the ray model is correct, then objects with a smooth edge should cast a sharp shadow, with a clear line between light and dark areas. When looking at a vertical-filament lightbulb through a small slit, the light spreads out to the sides, beyond the edges of the slit. If you did this, you also should have noticed a pattern of light and dark vertical lines, and even a few rainbows. I don't have the space here to explain that pattern, but the important fact is that the light spreads out. Coupled with the fact that light doesn't cast sharp shadows, this means that the ray model of light, although it's good for explaining many things, doesn't explain everything about the behavior of light. If light were rays that traveled in straight lines, then objects would cast sharp shadows, and light going through a narrow slit wouldn't spread out.

Before moving on to a different model of light, I just have to emphasize one of my pet peeves, which is that many textbooks and science resources claim that light travels in straight lines. That's consistent with the ray model of light, but it's just not true. Light "bends" around corners, just as sound does. We don't notice the bending every day because it isn't as pronounced as the bending of sound. We can hear around corners but we can't see around corners. But light doesn't travel in straight lines,

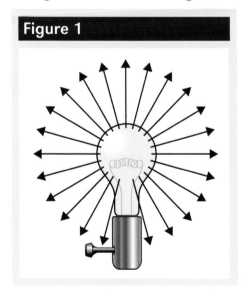

**Figure 1**

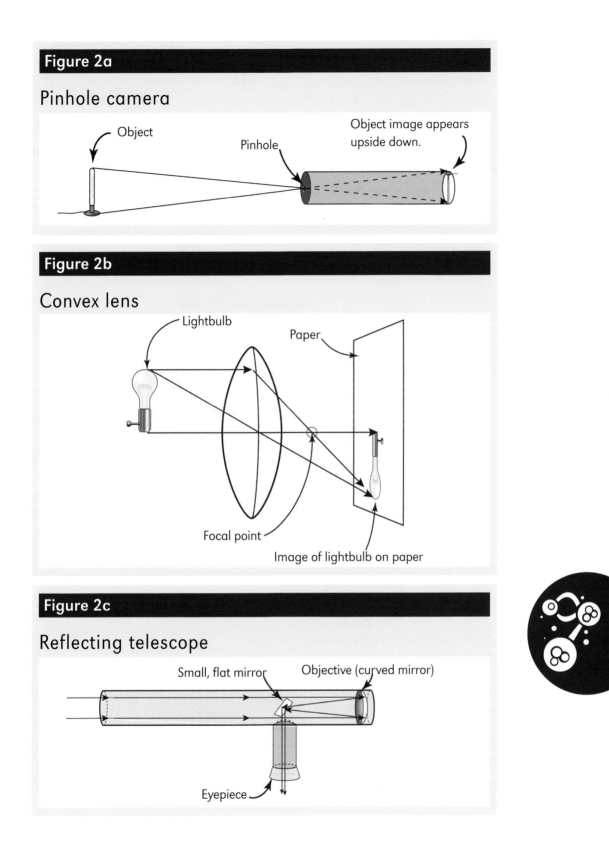

## Figure 2a

### Pinhole camera

Object

Pinhole

Object image appears upside down.

## Figure 2b

### Convex lens

Lightbulb

Paper

Focal point

Image of lightbulb on paper

## Figure 2c

### Reflecting telescope

Small, flat mirror

Objective (curved mirror)

Eyepiece

and science resources need to get that straight, so to speak. It's okay to use the ray model of light, but please explain the limitations of the model.

## The Other Models

Okay, so a ray model doesn't explain everything we observe. To explain our new observations, we have to look at light as a wave. The most direct way to see that light behaves as a wave is to mess around with water waves. Get a baking pan and fill it with water. Then place two objects in the pan close together so they create a small opening between them. Coffee cups will do for the two objects, and so will salt and pepper shakers. By tapping the water quickly with your finger, create water waves that will travel through the small opening created by your objects. See Figure 4.

As the waves pass through the small opening, you'll notice that the waves spread out. That's what waves do when they encounter barriers. Rays that travel in straight lines (as in light ray) don't do that. So, a different model of light is necessary to explain the fact that light spreads out when it encounters barriers. That model is—surprise—a wave model of light. The wave model of light isn't simple. It involves oscillations (vibrations) of electric fields and magnetic fields. Suffice to say that this model explains a bunch

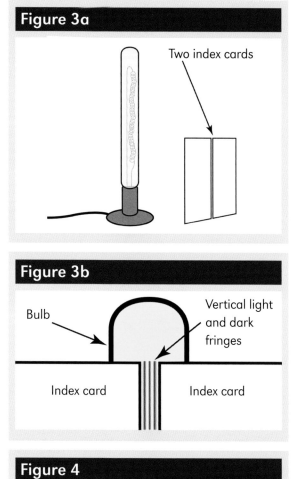

**Figure 3a**

Two index cards

**Figure 3b**

Bulb

Vertical light and dark fringes

Index card          Index card

**Figure 4**

## Salt and pepper shakers create a small opening for waves to pass through.

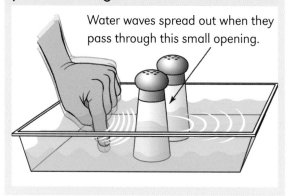

Water waves spread out when they pass through this small opening.

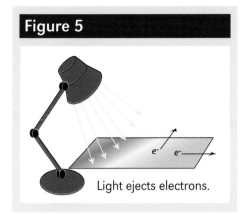

**Figure 5**

Light ejects electrons.

of observations that the ray model of light doesn't explain.

So now we have the right scientific model for light, right? There's another observation regarding light that indicates the need for a third model besides rays and waves. I'm going to describe the results of an experiment that you just can't do at home or in school, even though the results are crucial for our model of light. You'll just have to trust me regarding the results of the experiment. Anyway, here is the setup. You shine light on a piece of metal. This causes electrons to be ejected from the metal, as shown in Figure 5.

Now, this all makes sense if you know what atoms are like. They have a positively charged nucleus with negatively charged electrons around the nucleus. If you add energy to an atom (maybe by shining light on it), then you might give the electrons enough energy to escape the nucleus. Those electrons escape not just a nucleus but the metal altogether. This is called the *photoelectric effect.*

But this photoelectric effect has an unexpected result. When you shine high-energy (high-frequency) light on the metal, electrons jump off. But if you shine low-energy (low-frequency) light on the metal, you don't get any electrons. If the

wave model of light is correct, though, you should get electrons if you shine low-energy light on the metal long enough or with a high-intensity bright light. The electrons should leave the metal once they absorb enough of the low-energy light.

Let's try an analogy to explain why a wave model doesn't explain the photoelectric effect. Suppose you're on a beach, and you want to lift a heavy rock. You're going to do this by tying the rock to a rope, which goes over a pulley and is attached to a bucket placed above the beach where the surf comes in. As waves come in, they splash water into the bucket. Once there's enough water in the bucket, the weight of the water plus bucket lifts the rock up. If you have high-frequency waves, they come into the beach rapidly, one right after another. This fills up the bucket quickly, raising the rock. If you have low-frequency waves, they're spaced farther apart and don't fill the bucket up quickly. If you wait long enough, though, you will eventually have enough water in the bucket to raise the rock. Thus, both low-frequency and high-frequency waves lift the rock, but low-frequency waves take longer. Now, if the light involved in ejecting electrons from metal were simply waves like our water waves, both low-frequency light waves and high-frequency light waves would eventually provide enough energy to eject electrons from the metal; it would just take the low-frequency waves longer to do it. But that doesn't happen. There is a cutoff frequency below which the light doesn't eject electrons, no matter how long you wait. Light must not be behaving like waves in this instance.

The photoelectric effect, along with other experiments, led to a new model of light—the particle model. Light particles are called *photons*, and their energy is

proportional to the frequency of the light. Besides making photon torpedoes possible on the *USS Enterprise*, this model explains the photoelectric effect. Atoms can only absorb one photon at a time. If that one photon has enough energy, it can release electrons from the atom. Because photon energy is proportional to the frequency of the light, low-frequency light can never eject electrons from metal. No matter how many photons impact on the atoms of the metal, and no matter how long they go at it, the individual photons in low-frequency light just don't have enough energy to eject electrons (Figure 6).

Again, let's go back to our problem of lifting a rock. Instead of using water waves and a bucket, we're going to ask people passing by to lift the rock for us. Only one person at a time can attempt to lift the rock. So you could have 2,000 weak people pass by and try to lift the rock, and none will be successful. The rock doesn't budge. One strong person, though, will be able to lift the rock. The weak people are like low-frequency photons. No matter how many people try, you can't lift the rock. The strong people are like high-frequency photons. Each strong person can lift the rock, just as each high-frequency electron can eject an electron. This is what happens with the photoelectric effect. Low-frequency light can't eject electrons no matter how long you wait or how intense the light is. High-frequency light can eject electrons immediately, even at low intensities. So in this case,

light acts like particles (individual weak and strong people lifting the rock) rather than like waves.

Of course, the photon model of light explains a lot more than the photoelectric effect. For one thing, it's consistent with our model of the atom, which includes electrons residing only in discreet energy levels and emitting or absorbing photons when they (the electrons) jump from one level to another.

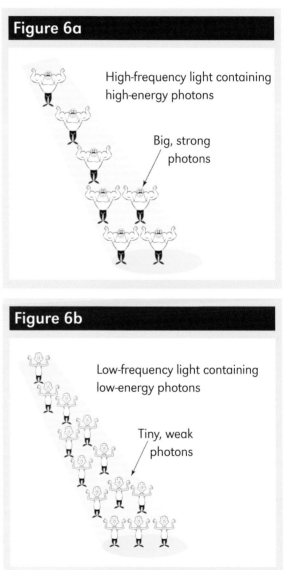

**Figure 6a**

High-frequency light containing high-energy photons

Big, strong photons

**Figure 6b**

Low-frequency light containing low-energy photons

Tiny, weak photons

National Science Teachers Association

## More Is Sometimes Better

Okay, so we have three models of light. Isn't one of them correct and the others wrong? Not really. The ray model of light is the best model to use when figuring out what lenses and mirrors will do, but it's clearly no good when dealing with situations where light spreads out, when adding and subtracting colors, and in other instances. In other cases, the wave model of light falls apart and the photon model is best. But the photon model doesn't help you figure out how a pair of glasses (a set of lenses) improves your vision. So all three models are correct, though each has limitations.

Having more than one scientific model for phenomena isn't limited to light. Newton's second law is one of the cornerstones of scientific explanations, but it has to be altered to describe things that move at speeds near the speed of light. And another theory (general relativity) completely takes over with systems on the scale of the universe. That doesn't make Newton's second law wrong. It just places limitations on its uses. Of course, scientists would prefer that one single model explain all observations, but that isn't always the case. ■

# Q: How do atomic clocks work?

A: In the early 1980s I was a starving graduate student in Boulder, Colorado. I was rescued from my part-time job as a line cook by an offer to conduct tours of the Bureau of Standards (now known as the National Institute of Standards), located in Boulder. One of the highlights of the tour was showing people the atomic clocks that kept our standard time. For many people, seeing the clocks was a bit of a letdown. I'm pretty sure they were expecting a dramatic display of radioactive devices, but instead they found long canisters just sitting there, doing their thing. Not even a radiation warning! The reason for that, of course, is that atomic clocks do not depend in any way on radioactive decay. Once the people on the tour found out how the clocks worked, though, they gained back a little enthusiasm because the operation of the clocks is pretty amazing.

You might be wondering why in the world we need such precise measures of time. Well, many systems we use every day, such as Global Positioning Systems, require precise synchronization of time. This comes into play in telecommunications

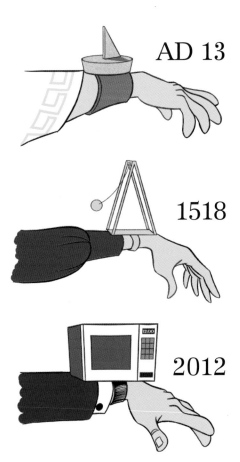

AD 13

1518

2012

Timepieces through history

## Figure 1

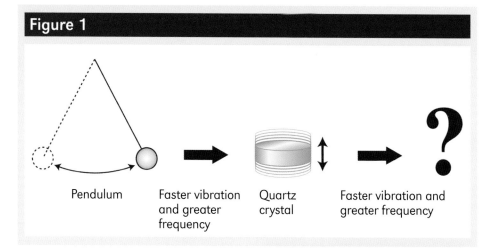

Pendulum — Faster vibration and greater frequency — Quartz crystal — Faster vibration and greater frequency — ?

and wireless communications as well. For purely scientific reasons, we can use precise measurement of time to determine whether or not fundamental constants in the universe appear to be changing over time. Not something that keeps the average person awake at night, but a big deal to theoretical physicists.

## Measuring Time

Before addressing atomic clocks, I have to discuss the ways we measure time. Whether the time we're measuring is long or short, we use anything that occurs at regular intervals. We measure a year's worth of time by how long it takes for the Earth to go around the Sun once. We measure a month by how long it takes for the Moon to go around the Earth once. For shorter time intervals, we could just break the year and month into tiny fractions, but that introduces a lot of error in the measurement. If you define a day as 1/365 of a year, and then an hour as 1/24 of a day, and then a second as 1/3600 of an hour, your definition of a second isn't very precise. This is analogous to trying to cut a cake into a million separate pieces that are exactly the same size. To get a better definition of a

## Figure 2

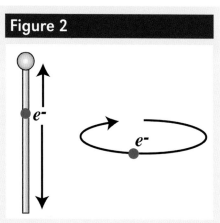

second, you could look at something such as how long it takes a simple pendulum to go back and forth once. Because the thing you're observing (the time for a pendulum to move back and forth) is much shorter than, say, a year, you can be more precise in how long a second is. That's why pendulum clocks keep better time than sundials. The smaller the measurement that determines the standard, the more precisely we can determine it. In our cake example, we'll have better luck getting our million pieces to be of equal size if we combine pieces of cake that are actually smaller than a single one of those million pieces. To keep better time than a pendulum clock, you need something that happens in a shorter time than it takes a pendulum to move back and forth. Quartz watches rely on the vibration of a quartz crystal to define what a second is. Quartz crystals vibrate really fast, so we have a smaller period of time (the time for a vibration of a quartz crystal) on which to base our measurement of time.

Following this logic, then, the way to get a really, really good measurement of time is to find a faster vibration than you get with a quartz crystal (see Figure 1). And for future reference in this discussion, the rate at which something vibrates (how many full oscillations per second) is called the *frequency of vibration.*

Enter electromagnetic waves, which include radio waves, microwaves, visible light, and ultraviolet waves. Our model of electromagnetic waves is that they are composed of vibrating electric and magnetic fields, and the vibrations are incredibly fast. All we need to do is find a way to measure how fast electromagnetic waves vibrate, and we'll have a very short time period on which to base our measurement of time. That's easier said than done, but before I explain how we do it, I have to discuss ways of generating electromagnetic waves.

## Electromagnetic Waves

There are two ways to look at the generation of electromagnetic

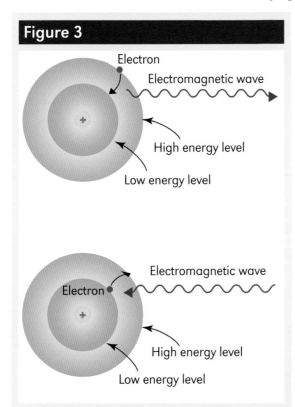

Figure 3

Electron

Electromagnetic wave

High energy level

Low energy level

Electromagnetic wave

Electron

High energy level

Low energy level

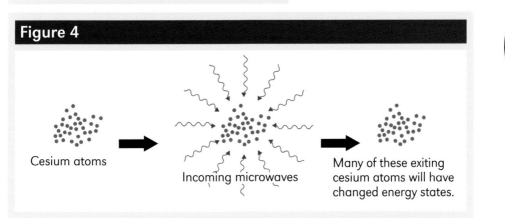

Figure 4

Cesium atoms

Incoming microwaves

Many of these exiting cesium atoms will have changed energy states.

waves. One way to do it, which only works for waves that vibrate slower than visible light waves, is to make electrons vibrate or move in circles. This is how we generate radio waves and is one way to generate microwaves (Figure 2, p. 140).

The other way to look at the generation of electromagnetic waves is to follow what happens to electrons within atoms. The electrons in atoms reside in distinct energy levels, and the allowed energy levels are dictated by the kind of atom. I can't go into *why* electrons reside in distinct energy levels here, but I've addressed that in a previous column. Anyway, electrons can jump from energy level to energy level within an atom. When they jump from a higher energy level to a lower energy level, they give off electromagnetic waves. When an electromagnetic wave of just the right

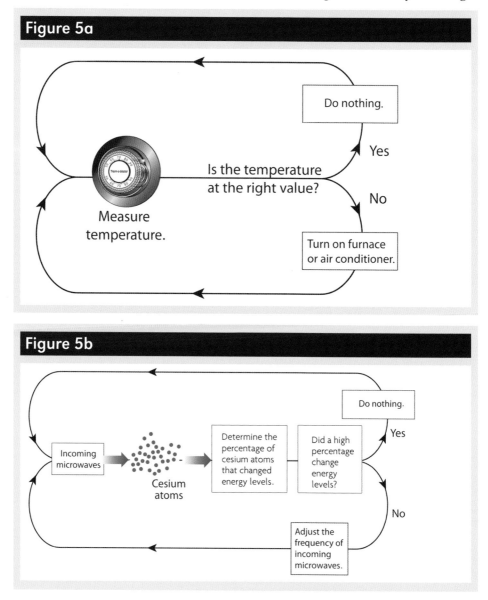

**Figure 5a**

Measure temperature.

Is the temperature at the right value?

Yes — Do nothing.

No — Turn on furnace or air conditioner.

**Figure 5b**

Incoming microwaves

Cesium atoms

Determine the percentage of cesium atoms that changed energy levels.

Did a high percentage change energy levels?

Yes — Do nothing.

No — Adjust the frequency of incoming microwaves.

energy (and frequency) runs into an atom, it can cause an electron to jump from a lower energy level to a higher energy level (Figure 3, p. 141).

## On to Clocks

Now we're ready to understand atomic clocks. The first atomic clock used an ammonia molecule for tuning microwave frequencies, but scientists discovered that the element cesium worked much better for this purpose. A cesium clock is based on the microwaves emitted by a certain transition of electrons between energy levels in a cesium-133 atom. To start with, you need a supply of cesium atoms. You send these atoms into a cavity, into which you send microwaves. These microwaves are generated by causing electrons to accelerate, which is basically how your microwave oven works. If the frequency of the incoming microwaves exactly matches the frequency that corresponds to the difference in energy levels of that transition in cesium, then the cesium atoms you have in the cavity will change from the lower energy state to the higher energy state. Figure 4 (p. 141) sketches this process. As you look at this and later diagrams, keep in mind that I'm showing you the overall process and that these diagrams don't correspond to the actual physical setup of an atomic clock.

If our generated microwaves exactly match the proper frequency to cause cesium-133 atoms to go from a lower energy state to a higher energy state, then many of the cesium atoms you put into the cavity will make the transition. The reason all of them won't make the transition is that the necessary frequency varies just a bit from atom to atom, depending on the motion of the atom at the time. What you do is take a look at the atoms that exit the cavity and figure out how many made the transition. If the percentage is high, you're just about on the right frequency. If the percentage is low, then you adjust the frequency of your incoming microwaves until you get a higher percentage of cesium-133 atoms making the transition. This is a lot like how a thermostat in your home works, with the thermostat checking the temperature and turning the furnace or air conditioner on or off depending on how close you are to the desired temperature. Figure 5 shows the process for thermostats and cesium clocks.

So instead of directly measuring the frequency of the microwaves emitted or absorbed by cesium-133, an atomic clock *matches* the frequency of microwaves aimed at cesium atoms to the proper frequency. Once that frequency is known, it can be used as a basis for determining how long a second is. Our current definition of the time period of a second is that it's 9,192,631,770 vibrations of the microwaves emitted or absorbed by cesium-133. Again, though, we don't measure the microwaves emitted by cesium-133 directly. We determine the frequency of microwaves generated by a separate source that cause cesium-133 atoms to undergo a transition from low to high energy. Of course, besides defining what a second is, atomic clocks can use the accurate measurement of microwave vibrations to determine the time of day with incredible precision.

The National Institute of Standards has developed many cesium clocks over the years, with each one being more accurate than the previous one. The first cesium clock gained or lost no more than a second in about 600 years. The newest cesium clock in use by the Institute of Standards gains or loses no more than one second in 60 million years. The Institute's latest

clock, known as a "cesium fountain" clock, uses lasers to compact the cesium atoms and cause them to spend more time in the microwave cavity than previous clocks did. It does this by tossing the compacted cesium up in the air and letting it fall back down—hence the fountain reference. More time in the microwave cavity means more time to refine the microwave frequency to obtain the maximum number of cesium atoms jumping from lower energy to higher energy. Of course, things keep improving. Just this year, physicists have developed an atomic clock using the element strontium rather than cesium, and this clock will gain or lose no more than a second in 200 million years!

I'll end with a couple of nice-to-know facts. First, you can buy what are known as atomic clocks for relatively little money. The reason they don't cost much is that they're not cesium clocks. They are simply clocks that are synchronized with the time signal put out by the National Institute of Standards. You can synchronize the clock on your computer with standard time and thus have an atomic clock right in front of you. The second fun thing to know is that the Institute of Standards adds "leap seconds" to the official time every once in a while. This is because the rotation of the Earth is slowing down due to tidal effects caused by the Sun and Moon. Thus, the day is getting longer (though not by much!). To correct for this slowing down, we have to add a second to the day every few years. You need more time in the day? You got it. ■

# Q: What causes the different states of matter?

A: The answer to this could be really simple or really complicated, depending on how deeply we cover the issue. I'll dispense with the really complicated by limiting the discussion to solids, liquids, and gases. There are many other states of matter, including plasmas, superfluids, and Bose-Einstein condensates(!), but you'll have to look up those other states of matter elsewhere. Even though we're staying simple, you might get a surprise or two, such as the fact that it's possible for iron to be a gas, and it's possible to have liquid or even solid hydrogen.

## It's the Molecules

People's knowledge of the states of matter often is limited to the characteristics of the states. Solids have a definite shape, liquids have a definite volume but take the shape of their container, and gases change their volume to fit their container. Besides the fact that these characteristics don't apply in all cases (glass, for instance, is a solid but

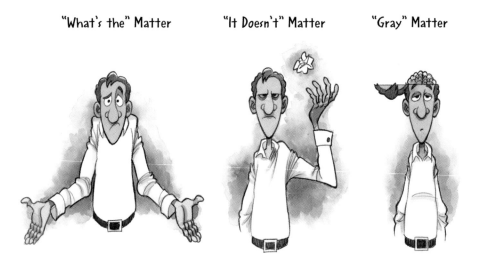

"What's the" Matter        "It Doesn't" Matter        "Gray" Matter

still acts like a fluid over long periods of time), they don't provide a model of what's going on in each state of matter. So we're going to look at how molecules behave in each state and how and why they change from one state to another.

It will help a lot if you try something before reading the explanation. Head to a craft store and get a couple of rubber or plastic balls (around 3 to 5 centimeters in diameter, but anything close to that will work) and a package of stick-on (with adhesive) magnets. If the magnets you buy are sufficiently cheap, they'll attract one another in just about any orientation. This is a good thing. You don't want magnets that repel strongly in certain orientations. Once you have your cheap magnets, attach them to each of the balls as shown in Figure 1. You don't have to exactly match the pattern shown there; just make sure you have a bunch of magnets distributed along the surface of each ball.

Now make the magnet balls crash into each other on a smooth surface. Do this with the balls moving slowly and then with the balls moving quickly. Then with the balls stuck together, push one of the balls gently and then with a lot of force. Hopefully, you get the results illustrated in Figure 2. (As an aside, I tried this activity using stick-on Velcro instead of magnets, and you don't get the necessary results. The balls stick together with Velcro no matter how hard you smash them into each other.)

Assuming our magnetic balls represent atoms or molecules, we can first model the three states of matter. When the balls (atoms or molecules) move around at high speeds, hit one another, and don't stick together, you have a gas. When the balls (atoms or molecules) stick together, yet you can still cause them to move around (and stay stuck) with a gentle push, that's a liquid. If you imagine that you have really strong magnets that don't allow the balls (atoms or molecules) to move much even when you push them, you have a solid.

Now let's focus on a couple of things that determine whether or not the atoms or molecules get together and stay together. The first thing is speed. As you should have noticed with the magnetic balls, the faster they were moving, the less likely they were to stick together. Atoms and molecules behave the same way. Faster moving atoms and molecules might collide, but they don't stick together in those collisions. So it would seem that for a bunch of atoms or molecules to be a gas, you have to make them move quickly. That's generally true. And it might make sense that when you increase the *temperature* of those atoms or molecules, they'll move faster. So if you increase the temperature of your atoms or molecules enough, you can cause them to be in the

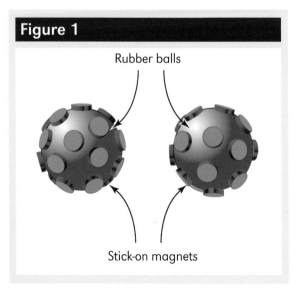

**Figure 1**

Rubber balls

Stick-on magnets

gaseous state. By lowering the temperature, you can cause the atoms or molecules to move slowly enough that their attraction is significant, and they stay together even though they can still move around a fair amount. That's a liquid. Even lower temperatures with less movement and more of a rigid structure give you a solid.

## Temperature, Too

That's only half the story with temperature. Temperature is not just a measure of speed, but a measure of the average *kinetic energy* of the molecules. The kinetic energy of an object is equal to $1/2mv^2$, where $m$ is the mass of the object and $v$ is the speed of the object. Let's apply this to a collection of molecules, some of which are massive and some of which are not so massive. If these molecules are all at the same temperature, then they all have the same average kinetic energy. Because kinetic energy involves mass as well as speed, however, the more massive molecules will have a lower average speed than the less massive molecules. See Figure 3 (p. 148).

This means that you could have a bunch of massive molecules at a high temperature that have a relatively low speed. With respect to states of matter, that means that it's harder to cause massive molecules to become a gas (which requires high speeds) and relatively easy to cause not-so-massive molecules to become a gas.

Grab yourself a periodic table and look at the elements at the top of the table, namely hydrogen and helium. The elements at the top of the table have a smaller mass than the elements at the bottom of the table, so you might expect the ones at the top to be gases at, say, room temperature. And they are. In fact, many of the elements you know to be gases at room temperature (oxygen, nitrogen, fluorine) are also near the top of the periodic table and therefore less massive.

## And Attraction

We don't have a complete picture, though. Carbon is less massive

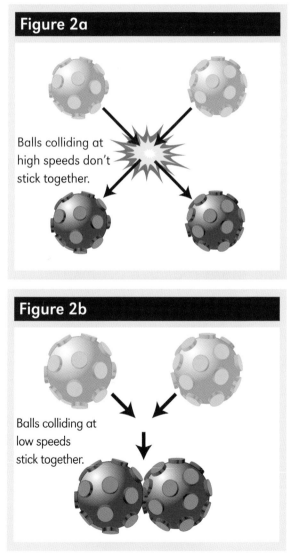

**Figure 2a**

Balls colliding at high speeds don't stick together.

**Figure 2b**

Balls colliding at low speeds stick together.

than oxygen, yet carbon is a solid at room temperature. The noble gases—the ones in the far right column of the periodic table (helium, neon, argon, etc.)—are all gases at room temperature even though many of them are quite heavy. To make sense of this, let's go back to our magnetic ball analogy. There, speed was important in determining whether or not the balls would stick together. If we were to change the strength of the magnets, though, that would also have an effect. If the magnets were extremely weak, the balls wouldn't stick together, no matter how slowly they were moving. If the magnets were extremely strong, the balls would stick together even when they hit each other at high speeds. So how strongly the balls (or molecules and atoms) interact is going to affect what state they are in. This helps us understand, for instance, why those noble gases toward the bottom of the periodic table can be gases even though they're quite massive and thus move more slowly than other atoms at a given temperature. For reasons that go a bit beyond what we're covering here, the noble gases are quite happy with the number of electrons they have (they have "filled electron shells") and thus interact little, if at all, with other atoms. So you can slow these guys down a whole bunch and they still won't stick together enough to form a liquid.

Now let's see what happens with carbon and oxygen. They have close to the same mass, yet one tends to be a solid at room temperature and the other tends to be a gas. The reason for this has to do with how strongly the atoms or molecules interact. Oxygen atoms readily combine with other oxygen atoms to form an oxygen molecule, designated as $O_2$. Once they have formed into oxygen molecules, they no longer readily interact with other oxygen molecules, so you have to get them to really low temperatures before they turn from gas to liquid. Carbon atoms, although they can join up with other carbon atoms, do not become less interactive once they do so. So at room temperature, you would still expect a bunch of carbon atoms to latch onto one another and become not just liquid, but solid. For the record, the situation with hydrogen is the same as with oxygen. Two hydrogen atoms get together to

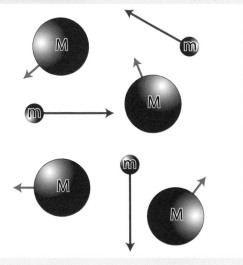

**Figure 3**

All of these are at the same temperature, but the less massive atoms (m) have a greater average speed than the more massive atoms (M).

form a hydrogen molecule, and hydrogen molecules don't interact much with other hydrogen molecules. Thus, hydrogen is a gas even at low temperatures.

## Water Is Special

For one more example, consider our favorite state of matter changer—water. We can have ice, water, and water vapor. What makes water a bit special is that water molecules (two hydrogens and an oxygen—$H_2O$) are *polar*, meaning that they have positive and negative sides. Because water is polar, it's more interactive with other molecules of water (electric attraction) than oxygen molecules are interactive with other oxygen molecules. So water becomes a liquid (individual water molecules in water vapor [the gaseous state] latch onto one another) more easily than oxygen and then becomes a solid more easily for the same reason. On the other hand, water molecules are less interactive than carbon molecules, so you need a lower temperature for water to become a solid than for carbon to become a solid.

## Oh, the Pressure

Before going on, I need to mention one more factor that affects the states of matter. That's pressure. If you increase the pressure on a gas or liquid while keeping the temperature the same, you are increasing the number of times the individual molecules collide. The way to do this without changing temperature is to decrease the volume. Imagine you have a box of oxygen molecules and you make the box smaller and smaller without making the mol-

ecules move faster. In making the box smaller, you increase the number of times the molecules bump into one another. That increases the prob-

Topic: States of Matter
Go to: *www.scilinks.org*
Code: ASQ022

ability that they'll stick together and form a liquid.

Changing temperature and pressure is how people create liquid nitrogen, liquid helium, liquid oxygen, and liquid hydrogen. You get these gases to *extremely* low temperatures and then increase the pressure until you get a liquid. Carrying this process further can result in bizarre things like solid hydrogen. On the other side of the scale, you can create gases out of things we normally consider solids by increasing the temperature and reducing pressure (less pressure means fewer collisions). So you can heat up iron until it's liquid iron (you've no doubt seen this in videos of steel-making), then heat some more and also reduce the pressure around the liquid iron to create iron vapor. For the record, you can use iron vapor to isolate individual iron atoms for study, and scientists have recently created an iron vapor laser.

To sum up, whether something is a solid, liquid, or gas depends on how strongly the atoms or molecules are connected to one another. Many things can affect how strongly they're connected. The temperature, the mass, the speed, the strength of interaction, and the pressure all affect the states of matter. Hopefully you now know *how* those things affect the states of matter. ■

# Q: What makes a curveball curve?

A: Ah, springtime, and young people's thoughts turn to ... baseball, of course. I remember spending a lot of time trying to throw a curveball when I was playing Little League baseball, and after doing a bit of research, I now know that I was doing it wrong and why all I did was hurt my elbow. But this column is not about *how* to throw a curveball, so you'll have to look that up on your own. Here I'll focus on the *why* of the curveball.

For starters, you should throw a curveball yourself—the easy way. Get a cardboard paper-towel tube (sans paper towels) and a Ping-Pong ball. Hold one end of the tube and place the Ping-Pong ball inside

Wow! That's a **mean** curveball.

the tube so it's at the end near your hand. Swing the tube to the side. With a bit of practice, you can do this so the Ping-Pong ball comes out the far end of the tube and travels across the room. It should also curve dramatically. Once you master this, see if you can figure out what the ball is doing as it exits the tube. If you can't figure that out, I'll tell you. The ball is spinning rapidly as it exits. This is because as you swing the tube, you cause the ball to roll along one side of the tube (Figure 1).

So the way to make a ball curve is to have it spinning when you throw it. The reason a Ping-Pong ball curves so much is that it has a small mass, and effects from the air rushing by it are greater than for a baseball.

Figure 2 shows the relationship between the spin and the resulting curve for any kind of ball.

## Figure 1

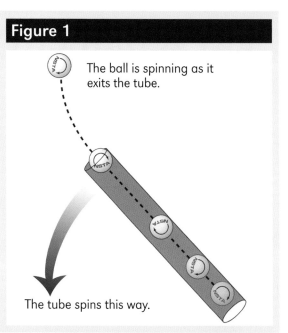

The ball is spinning as it exits the tube.

The tube spins this way.

## Figure 2

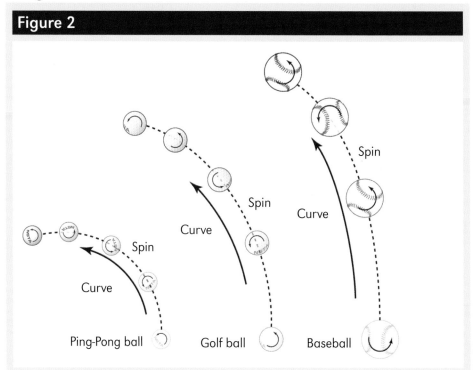

Ping-Pong ball    Golf ball    Baseball

**Figure 3**

There are two different things that cause a spinning ball to curve. One is known as the *Bernoulli effect* and the other is known as the *Magnus effect*. The Bernoulli effect is the easiest to understand, so I'll start with that, even though the Magnus effect is the dominant one in causing a ball to curve.

## The Bernoulli Effect

First, experience the Bernoulli effect by blowing across the top of a sheet of paper, as shown in Figure 3. The paper should rise up. This illustrates that the faster air moves, the lower the pressure. When you cause the air on top of the paper to move faster than the still air underneath the paper, that makes the air pressure below the paper higher than the air pressure on top of the paper. This pressure difference pushes the paper up (Figure 4). The relationship of air speed to pressure is called the *Bernoulli effect*. I would like to explain exactly *why* faster air speed means lower pressure, but there isn't room in this column. Perhaps you could find a book

that explains it well, such as the *Air, Water, and Weather* book in the Stop Faking It! series (shameless self-promotion).

Now let's apply the Bernoulli effect to a spinning baseball. As the baseball spins, it drags a thin layer of air with it. As Figure 5 (p. 154) shows, this results in the air on one side of the ball moving past the ball faster than the air on the opposite side of the ball. Because faster-moving air means a lower pressure, the difference in air pressure pushes the ball in the direction shown. Hence, a curveball.

## The Magnus Effect

Now, it turns out that the Bernoulli effect described above is a relatively minor reason why a curveball curves. The main reason it curves is known as the *Magnus effect*. To understand that effect, we have to investigate what are known as *boundary layers*. Think about air moving across a flat surface, as shown in Figure 6 (p. 154). The air right next to the surface actually comes to rest on the surface because of the friction between the surface and the air. As you move away

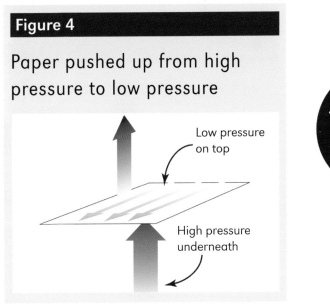

**Figure 4**

## Paper pushed up from high pressure to low pressure

Low pressure on top

High pressure underneath

from the surface, the air moves more and more relative to the surface, until the air moves at the regular speed of the air far away from the surface. This region between air at rest next to the surface and air moving at its regular speed is called the boundary layer of air.

On a round surface, such as that of a baseball, the boundary layer at some point separates from the surface of the ball, creating a "wake," not unlike a water wake from a boat. Figure 7 shows this wake for a ball traveling through air but not spinning.

When the boundary layer separates

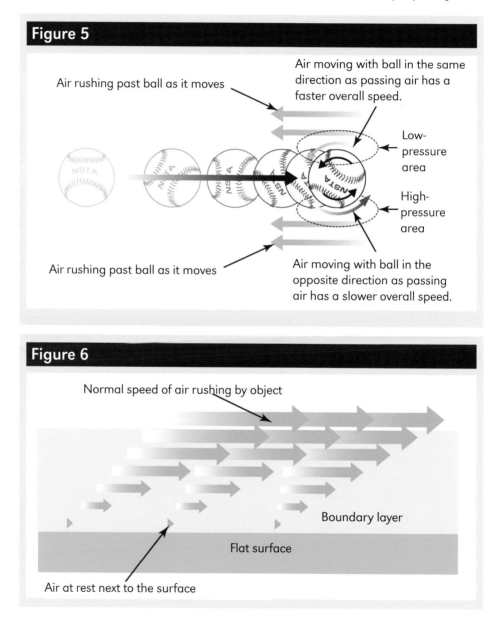

## Figure 5

Air rushing past ball as it moves

Air moving with ball in the same direction as passing air has a faster overall speed.

Low-pressure area

High-pressure area

Air rushing past ball as it moves

Air moving with ball in the opposite direction as passing air has a slower overall speed.

## Figure 6

Normal speed of air rushing by object

Boundary layer

Flat surface

Air at rest next to the surface

from the ball, it's a lot like the ball is *throwing* the layer of air backward. And as all of us who understand Newton's third law know, when you throw something in one direction, that something pushes back on you in the opposite direction. Thus, the separation of the boundary layer actually pushes the ball forward.

On to a spinning ball that's heading toward home plate. Because the passing air is moving in the direction of spin on one side of the ball, this delays the separation of the boundary layer from the ball. It speeds up the separation on the other side of the ball. The result is shown in Figure 8 (p. 156). The "wake" is shifted from straight backward to the side.

So instead of "throwing" the boundary layer straight backward, as happens with a non-spinning ball, a spinning ball throws the boundary layer off to the side a bit. This, because of Newton's third law, pushes the ball sideways: a curveball.

Having had to read several descriptions of the Magnus effect several times, I understand that it's a difficult concept. So feel free to reread this column a couple of times before deciding you don't understand it. In the meantime, I'll share with you a really bad description of what makes curveballs curve. While reading an article on the Colorado Rockies (Colorado's Major League Baseball team) in a major sports magazine, I encountered an explanation of why pitchers have a difficult time throwing curveballs in Denver. The explanation was that because Denver is a mile above sea level, the gravitational force of the Earth on objects is less than it is at sea level. Thus, curveballs don't "drop" as fast in Denver.

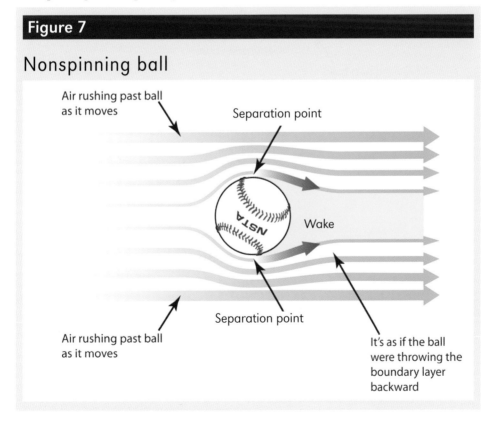

## Figure 7

## Nonspinning ball

Air rushing past ball as it moves

Separation point

Wake

Separation point

Air rushing past ball as it moves

It's as if the ball were throwing the boundary layer backward

Nonsense. The Earth's gravitational force is definitely less at a mile high than at sea level, but the difference is insignificant for the path of a curveball. What *is* significant is that, at higher elevations, the density of the air is much lower. Thinner air means less of an effect from either Bernoulli or Magnus. I wrote a letter to this major sports magazine regarding the error, but they ignored me. Silly sports magazine. ■

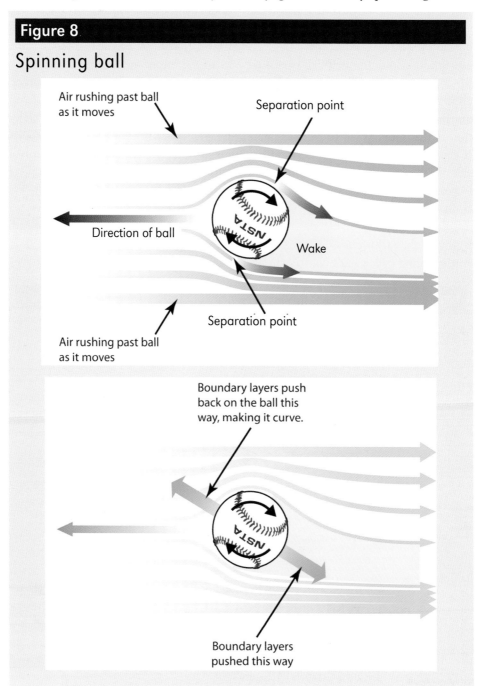

**Figure 8**

## Spinning ball

Air rushing past ball as it moves

Separation point

Direction of ball

Wake

Separation point

Air rushing past ball as it moves

Boundary layers push back on the ball this way, making it curve.

Boundary layers pushed this way

National Science Teachers Association

# How does a telescope work?

It turns out that telescopes, microscopes, and binoculars all work on the same principles, so you get three for one in this answer. In each case, we are engaged in what you might call "remote viewing." We use microscopes to view things that are very small. We're close enough to them to see them, but we're not small enough to see them. Therefore, we use a microscope to make things like amoebas look larger than they are. Objects in the heavens are certainly large enough for us to see them, but they're really far away. So we use telescopes to make these objects appear closer than they are. Pretty much the same thing with binoculars. We use them to view things that we could normally see just fine, but that are too far away. Again, we make the image larger.

# A Lens on Lenses

With similar purposes, you would expect these three instruments to have similar components, and by golly they do. I'll address telescopes since that's the focus of the question. The first thing you need for remote viewing is a component that gathers light from the object you're viewing. This component is known as the *objective*. For telescopes, the objective is either a lens or a mirror. To get an idea of how objectives work, grab a flashlight, a spoon, and a magnifying glass or pair of glasses used by a far-sighted person.

Shine your flashlight on any surface. Then place either a magnifying lens or a glasses lens (for far-sighted folk) between the flashlight and the surface. Adjust the positions of these objects until you manage to get a bright spot on the surface. This bright spot should be brighter than you can get with just the flashlight alone. See Figure 1.

Next shine your flashlight on the spoon as shown in Figure 2. Adjust things until you once again get a bright spot that is brighter than what you can get with the flashlight alone.

As you just observed, lenses or curved mirrors (a spoon is a crude curved mirror) can gather light and focus it in a small area. The objective in a telescope does the same thing. It gathers light from stars, planets, etc., and focuses the light. A telescope that uses a lens for this purpose is called a *refracting telescope* (because the lens bends, or *refracts*, the incoming light), and a telescope that uses a mirror to focus incoming light is called a *reflecting telescope* (because the mirror reflects the incoming light). Figure 3 (p. 162) shows partial drawings of a reflecting telescope and a refracting telescope.

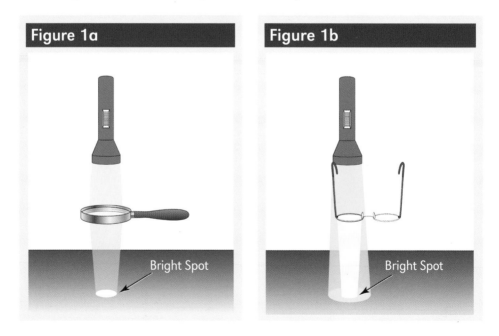

**Figure 1a**

Bright Spot

**Figure 1b**

Bright Spot

## Figure 2

# Bending basics

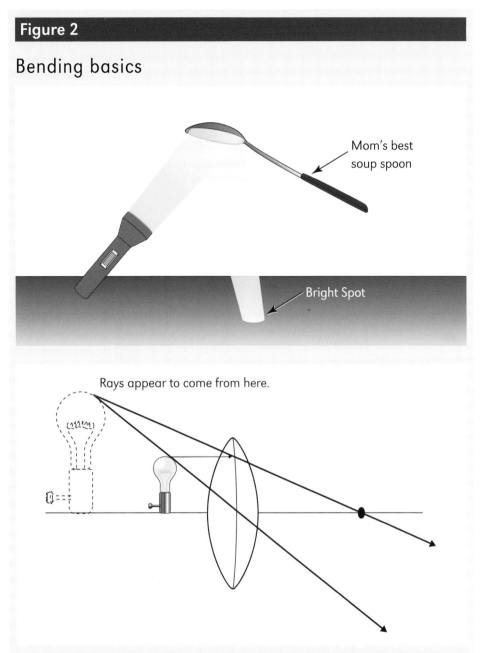

Mom's best soup spoon

Bright Spot

Rays appear to come from here.

The lens in the magnifying glass bends the light rays coming from the lightbulb in the drawing. The actual light rays are solid lines. This bending makes it appear to a viewer to the right of the lens that the light rays from the lightbulb are coming from a much larger lightbulb. The dotted lines show where the light rays appear to be coming from. Thus, the viewer to the right of the lens sees a magnified image of the lightbulb. Using this same process, the eyepiece of a telescope magnifies the image captured by the objective lens in the telescope.

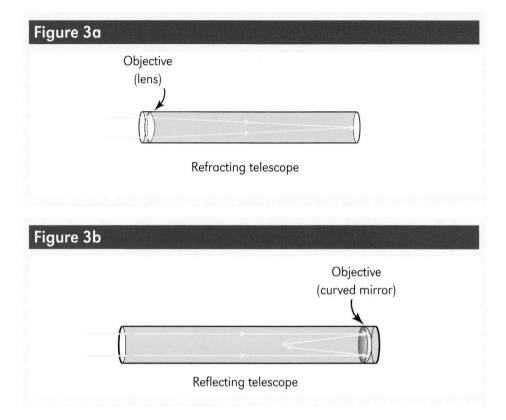

**Figure 3a**

Objective
(lens)

Refracting telescope

**Figure 3b**

Objective
(curved mirror)

Reflecting telescope

Okay, now we've used the objective lens or mirror to gather and focus light from the heavens. The image we get is much too small to see any detail. What we need is another lens that will magnify the image. This is called the *eyepiece*. The eyepiece in a telescope works just as a magnifying glass you use to make print look larger.

## Refracting Versus Reflecting

Anyway, we now have a complete picture of a telescope, whether refracting or reflecting. The objective gathers the light and the eyepiece magnifies the image produced by the objective. Check out Figure 4, which shows more complete drawings of a typical refracting telescope and a typical reflecting telescope.

The larger in diameter the objective lens or mirror in a telescope, the more light it can gather. More light gathered means a more detailed image of what you're looking at. Therefore, larger-diameter telescopes are better telescopes. Larger telescopes mean design problems, though. With a lens, the larger you make it, the more it weighs. At some point, the lens gets so large that it sags under its own weight. That makes a distorted lens, which isn't a good thing. So there's an upper limit on the size of a refracting telescope. The Yerkes Observatory in Wisconsin houses the largest refracting telescope in the world. The diameter of the lens in this telescope is 40 inches.

Reflecting telescopes are less troublesome, in part because they avoid the distortion inherent in using a lens to gather light and in part because you can make reflecting telescopes that gather more light.

## Figure 4a

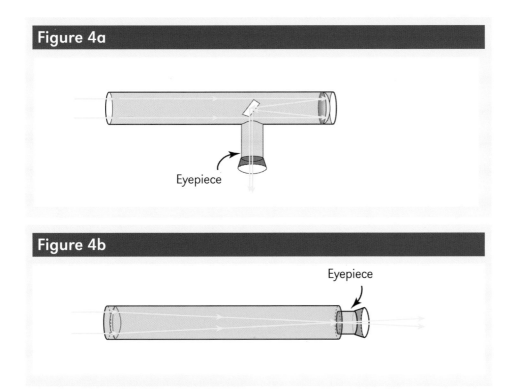

Eyepiece

## Figure 4b

Eyepiece

## Figure 5a

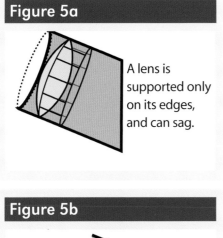

A lens is supported only on its edges, and can sag.

## Figure 5b

A mirror can be supported across its entire back surface.

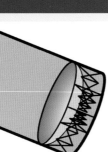

Because you only use one side of a mirror to focus light, you can support the mirror on the opposite side to keep it from sagging (Figure 5). Because of the difference in construction between the two types of telescopes, the most powerful telescopes around are reflecting telescopes. The largest reflecting telescope in the world, located at the Keck Observatory in Mauna Kea, Hawaii, has a diameter of 400 inches—much larger than the 40 inches for the largest refracting telescope. The Hubble Space telescope is also a reflector.

As I said in the beginning, telescopes, microscopes, and binoculars all use the same basic mechanism. Because size isn't a big issue with the latter two, they only use lenses rather than mirrors to gather light. Of course, microscopes and binoculars do use mirrors to change the direction light moves, but the mirrors aren't used

for gathering light or magnifying images. Binoculars also have extra components to make the images appear right side up, something that's not terribly important for telescopes and microscopes.

## Beyond Objects

Lest I leave you with the impression that telescopes use only visible light for viewing objects, I should mention radio telescopes. Radio telescopes gather radio waves emitted by astronomical objects and focus them for "viewing." Our eyes are not sensitive to radio waves, so what astronomers do is assign various colors to radio waves of different frequencies. They can then construct a "picture" that reveals the pattern of radio waves collected by the telescope. And yes, the radio waves we receive from stars, planets, and other such objects tell us more about the objects than visible light waves alone do. For example, matter that is not hot enough to emit light—and is therefore invisible to a light-gathering telescope—might be hot enough to emit radio waves and thus be "visible" using a radio telescope. And while I'm discussing nontraditional telescopes, I'll mention electron microscopes. Electron microscopes are *not* used for viewing electrons. Rather, an electron microscope fires electrons (rather than light) at an object and uses the pattern of reflected electrons to see detail on a scale impossible to see using a light microscope. For example, electron microscopes can actually give us an image of individual atoms in a substance. Not possible with visible light.

To summarize, all kinds of telescopes and microscopes give us information that we can't get with the unaided eye. To do that, these devices gather as much information (in the form of emitted light or other electromagnetic waves or in the form of reflected electrons) as possible, focus it in a small area, and then enlarge the result for easy viewing. Now, if we could just develop a similar system to find out what's going on in the mind of a teenager. ■

# How does wireless internet work?

Let's see … first you head to a coffee shop and order a mocha caramel chai latte with an extra shot of espresso. Then you turn on your computer, hit the connect button, and start surfing the web. For those who want more detail, read on. To understand how wireless internet (Wi-Fi) works, we need to address three main components—the modem, the router, and your computer.

## Modems

The purpose of a modem is to translate the information coming from your computer into a form that is suitable for phone lines

"Are you sure this is a *Wi-Fi* hot spot?"

and to translate information from phone lines into a form that your computer can understand. You might already know that computers use the binary number system, which is composed of ones and zeros. The reason computers use binary language is that ones and zeros are easy to represent with electric circuits, and your computer is composed of electric circuits. The way you do this with circuits is to make electric

## Figure 1

### A dial-up connection to the internet

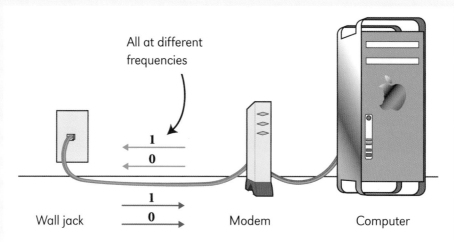

All at different frequencies

Wall jack     Modem     Computer

## Figure 2

### Wireless connection to the internet using a router

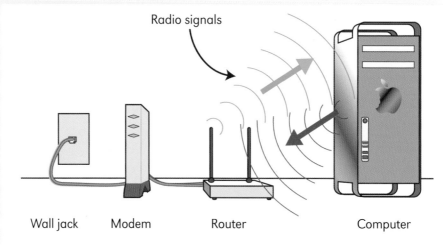

Radio signals

Wall jack     Modem     Router     Computer

**Figure 3**

## Dispersion of radio waves

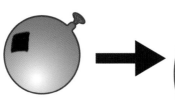

Radio signals spread out with distance the same way a square on a balloon spreads out as the balloon gets bigger.

switches. When a switch is on, it's a one, and when a switch is off, it's a zero.

Okay, so you have a modem and your computer can talk to the equipment at the internet service provider and vice versa. How can you send and receive signals at the same time? This is accomplished by using signals of different frequencies. Frequency is a measure of how many cycles, or signals, per second you send. Your computer and the provider's equipment can detect signals of different frequencies, just as a radio can detect signals of different frequencies corresponding to different radio stations. So a modem sends a 1 at one frequency and sends a 0 at a different frequency. The ones and zeros coming back to the modem are sent at two other frequencies. With these signals happening at four different frequencies, they can all be sent at once with no confusion (see Figure 1).

If you use a dial-up connection to the internet (you Neanderthal, you), then the modem you use is hard-wired into your computer. Just plug the phone line into the appropriate place on your computer, and you're set. If you want to go wireless, though, you need another piece of equipment.

## Routers

A router is an intermediary between your computer and a modem. Your computer communicates with the router, which communicates with the modem, which sends a signal over phone lines (or a satellite dish). The technology for this communication is an old one. We use radio waves. Your computer has a wireless card or wireless adapter that converts ones and zeros into radio waves. Then the router converts the radio waves back into ones and zeros and sends the information to the modem. The same process happens in reverse, so your computer can receive signals from the router. Figure 2 shows the communication process with a router involved.

Now, you don't want radio waves from your computer to interfere with the radio

waves you get on your radio, and vice versa. Different frequencies to the rescue again. AM radio uses frequencies in the kilohertz (1,000 cycles per second) range. FM radio uses frequencies in the megahertz (1,000,000 cycles per second) range, and routers and computers use signals in the gigahertz (1,000,000,000 cycles per second) range. Even though all these radio waves permeate the space around you, different electric circuits are built so as to receive particular frequencies and reject other frequencies. Your radio does this in a narrow range of frequencies when you change stations. An extra benefit of routers and computers using really high frequencies is that the higher the frequency, the more data per second you can transmit. More data per second means not waiting forever to open a web page.

Before moving on, I have something for you to do. Get a balloon and blow it up just a little bit. Hold the end but don't tie it off. Take a marker and draw a small square on the balloon. Then blow it up to at least twice the size and look at your square. You should get something like Figure 3 (p. 167).

The square spreads out considerably, no? Radio signals do the same thing. They spread out and become weaker the farther you are from the source. This is a good thing for the radio we listen to and a good thing for wireless internet service. If radio signals didn't dissipate quickly with distance, then radio signals from different parts of the country would interfere with one another and you'd get a jumbled mess. Of course, some radio stations emit stronger signals than others. You can hear major radio station signals across several states, while the local college station seldom reaches very far.

If you have a router in your home, you *want* the signal from the router and the signal from your computer to die out rather quickly. That way, the whole neighborhood doesn't access the internet via your router, and you don't broadcast to the neighborhood what you're doing on the internet. Wi-Fi "hot spots" also have a limited range. Your local coffee shop has Wi-Fi available so you come to the coffee shop to do your internet work and buy their caffeine. If the signal from their router extends two miles, you don't have to be in the coffee shop to access the router. Bad for business.

## Bunches of Users

At a wireless hot spot, be it a coffee shop, an airport, or a library, you have multiple users. How does the router (or series of routers in large-area hot spots) distinguish between all those signals coming in from different computers? Different frequencies, used by a modem and the phone line, won't work. For that to work, each computer would have to transmit at a different frequency, and the router would have to be able to accept all those frequencies. With everyone and his or her kids owning a laptop, the number of separate frequencies necessary would be overwhelming.

To understand how the routers keep track of things, first I'll address how your internet provider keeps track of, say, individual computers hooked up to the internet. If you connect directly to the internet, your computer is assigned an IP (internet protocol) address, which accompanies any packet of information you send and serves as a destination point for packets of information you receive. Think of it as an electronic "tag" that is assigned to the information. When you put a router in the chain of connections, the router itself has the IP address. So how does a multiple-use router at the airport keep track of individual computers? It uses a "dynamic" process by which it assigns its own IP address to each computer that signs up to use the router. The next time you sign on to this same router, you'll get a different address from the router. The router then can keep all of your computer's signals together in a packet and can even reject your computer's signal if you haven't paid the appropriate fee. Security on your home computer is achieved the same way. You can program your home router to accept only packets of information that contain the proper ID. ∎

# Index